Learn to Read
FLETCHER'S
PLACE
Game Book

Judy Kranzler & Cyndy Lemyre

Open
Reading

Play along with episodes at
OpenReading.com

ISBN 979-888896473-6

Graphic Design and Illustrations by
Valerie Bouthyette
Fedjine "Faye" Constant, Constant Creates LLC
Cyndy Lemyre

TABLE OF CONTENTS

Dear Parents, Teachers, Coaches and Friends,

We applaud you for taking a leading role in your children's education. It has been our life's mission to develop learn-to-read solutions that are entertaining and effective in ways that have never before been achieved. We are excited to bring you the culmination of that 40 years of experience in this program.

This is not like other learn-to-read programs

The Fletcher's Place episodes at OpenReading.com and this accompanying game book have been carefully constructed and thoroughly tested with thousands of children. Each episode breaks reading skills into step-by-step lessons, so no child gets left behind. Unlike other programs, Fletcher's Place engages a child's whole mind and body with physical play, music, fantasy, games, and exciting problem-solving activities. We continue to prove that children with all combinations of learning strengths love to learn this way.

In contrast, other programs gloss over key reading skills and are tedious, forcing children to "sit-look-and listen." They may advertise they're fun and full of play while, in fact, they consist of endless repetition, fill-in-the-blanks, and rote memorization. That said, some children can learn to read with flashcards and rote memory. Those "natural" readers have a strong "mental camera" and can memorize every word easily. But even those children prefer to learn with this play-based program.

Time and again parents delight as their children discover their own combination of learning strengths. So, in addition to reading confidence, children learn how they learn, something that will supercharge their success in school and life. Thank you in advance for trusting us with this most essential skill.

With love and conviction,
Judy Kranzler and Cyndy Lemyre

How to Use Fletcher's Place Game Book
for Parents & Teachers of Beginning Readers

OpenReading.com provides parents and teachers with free reading lessons which are so essential for beginning and struggling readers. These evidence-based lessons are couched in 10 entertaining kid-friendly episodes called Fletcher's Place.

Fletcher's Place keeps your busy schedule in mind by demonstrating the games on the video episodes. Then you can reinforce each reading skill with the hundreds of easy-to-use games.

Each page is a separate game with everything you need to play that game. Place the game pieces in envelopes so you can reuse them as many times as children want.

Cut out and keep handy the overview pages for each of the 10 episodes. These "cheat sheets" include a list of the:
- Reading skills
- Game selections
- Tips and reference materials
- The QR code to play that video episode

Tips to supercharge learning:

1. Children learn best by doing, not watching. Encourage children to get up, sing, and dance while watching. Challenge your children to answer Pockets (a character in the episodes) out loud.

2. Children need to watch each episode over and over. Repeat each episode until they have mastered the skills in that episode before moving on to the next one.

3. For most children, watching a whole episode in one sitting is not an effective way to learn. Instead, have them watch just a part of the episode at a time. Repeat each part as many times as they like as they play their way through the games for that episode.

Superpowers of Fletcher's Place

These are what make Fletcher's Place powerfully effective — but may feel most foreign to how we learned to read decades ago.

Break reading down into micro-skills and practice one at a time. Other programs teach a bunch of micro-skills all at once, frustrating children. For example teaching blending assuming children know the left-to-right reading direction can frustrate a child. This program teaches each micro-skill explicitly and one at a time.

Call letters by their most common sound, not letter names. Simply put, if you could reduce from 52 things to learn (26 letter names plus 26 letter sounds) to just 26 things that your child has to learn before they can start reading, why wouldn't you? Once children are confidently reading...letter names are taught in Episode 10.

Sound movements take advantage of how physically active children are. Sound movements are great memory hooks to learn the letter sounds and they make the skill of blending letter sounds together into words active and easy.

Note: These sound movements have been revolutionary in helping all children learn to read. They are open source to all curriculum developers to advance the entire industry of learn-to-read solutions. Learn more at OpenReading.com.

Stretch words out in slow motion to sound them out like this: *sssuuunnn*. Many children have difficulty recognizing a word when it is chopped apart like this: *sss....uuu....nnn*. Listen for this in the Episodes.

About the Authors

Judy Kranzler, Founder, Director of Pedagogy
Judy Kranzler has over 40 years of experience reviewing, developing and implementing reading and spelling curricula, materials, and multi-media for students with learning challenges, English Language Learners, as well as students who simply prefer to learn through physically active, musically vibrant, engaging activities.

Her personal experience of struggling with learning to read using the traditional "sit, look, listen, and memorize whole words," made her feel like she was learning disabled. By the time she finally felt she had mastered reading, she also knew in her heart that the way reading is traditionally taught discriminates against students who learn using other modalities other than the linguistic and visual methods.

Judy then studied and used many of the alternative ways to teach reading that were phonics and Orton-Gillingham-based. These methods teach a step-by-step progression of cumulative skills and teach the rules of how the sounds in English make words. She adapted these and melded them with her decades of experience helping children (and adults) to form the method we present to you today.

Cyndy Lemyre, Product Manager
Cyndy Lemyre is part of the curriculum development team for Open Reading, developing material for teaching reading to struggling readers of all ages for over 25 years.

As the Director (retired) as well as Academic Advisor, teacher trainer, and instructor at the Active Reading Center, the premier reading center in the San Francisco Bay Area, she brings her extensive success working with all students to bear in every detail of our program.

Fletcher's Place Left-to-Right Reading Arrow

-In Episodes 4-10 children train their eyes to read from left to right.

-Before beginning Episode 4, cut out a reading arrow from here or page 401. (For a sturdier arrow, glue it to cardboard.) Children use it to read letters, words, phrases and sentences.

-To use, place the arrow with the dog's head on the left under individual letters, words, phrases, and sentences. Children slide their pointer finger along the arrow from the dog to the bone as they read to guide their eyes left to right along the text.

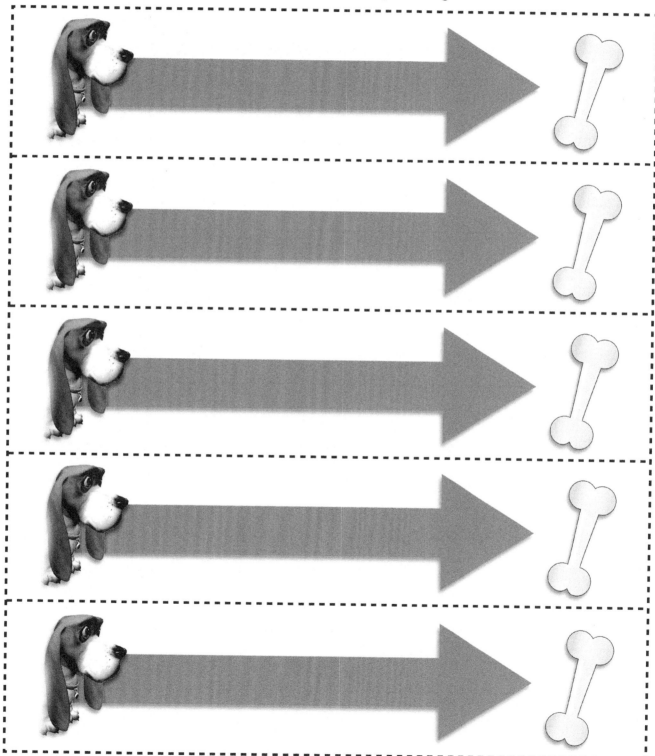

Blank Page

Episode 1: The Search for Treasure Hunt Island

Overview

Children use sound movements to learn the lowercase letter shapes and sounds for their first three letters. They learn the reading direction, the word "first," and learn to control eye movements.

Episode 1: We meet 4 friends who start learning to read in Fletcher's doghouse with his magical doll Pockets.

Quick Tip: Children learn best by doing. Encourage your child to get up, sing, and dance with the videos. Challenge your child to answer Pockets out loud.

Reading Skills

- Use sound movements to connect each letter's common sound to its lowercase shape for *i, n,* and *f.*
- Say "stretchy letter" sounds slowly and then say them fast.
- Learn the meaning of the word "first" when learning to read.
- Slide the pointer finger to pull eyes along letters for tracking text with ease.
- Describe the basic shapes needed to build letters: lines, circles, arcs, dips, and dots. (Pockets also calls these shapes sticks, circles, humps, curves and dots.)

Open video

New letter shapes, sounds, and sound movements

i <u>i</u>n

f o<u>ff</u>

n <u>on</u>

Sound Guide

a	-	<u>a</u>t
b	-	ro<u>b</u>
c	-	ki<u>ck</u>
d	-	o<u>dd</u>
e	-	<u>e</u>xit
f	-	o<u>ff</u>
g	-	<u>f</u>og
h	-	<u>h</u>ot
i	-	<u>i</u>t
j	-	<u>edge</u>
k	-	ki<u>ck</u>
ck	-	ki<u>ck</u>
l	-	hi<u>ll</u>
m	-	a<u>m</u>
n	-	o<u>n</u>
o	-	<u>o</u>ff
p	-	<u>up</u>
qu	-	<u>qu</u>it
r	-	hai<u>r</u>
s	-	u<u>s</u>
t	-	i<u>t</u>
u	-	<u>up</u>
v	-	lo<u>v</u>e
w	-	o<u>w</u>e
x	-	o<u>x</u>
y	-	happ<u>y</u>
z	-	bu<u>zz</u>
th	-	<u>th</u>is

Episode 1: The Search for Treasure Hunt Island

	Games to Play	Shown in Episode
1	Stretch and Snap Words	Ep. 1: Part 2
2	Match Game: Letters & Sound Movements	Ep. 1: Part 3
3	Read My Hands	Ep. 5: Part 2
4	Sound Bucket- First Sounds	Ep. 2: Part 3
5	Body Letter Shapes	Ep. 1: Part 3
6	Letter Puzzles	Ep. 1: Part 3
7	Slam	Ep. 1: Part 3
8	Find the Hidden Picture	not shown
9	Finger Slide	Ep. 1: Part 3

Tips

Why explicitly teach the words "first" and "last?"
To understand the vocabulary of reading instruction, Fletcher's Place uses "first" and "last" to refer to letters at the beginning or end of words. Practice with children using the words "first" and "last" in everyday situations.

Why teach letter sounds now, and not letter names?
Children only need each letter's common sound to start reading. This cuts in half what children need to learn and eliminates a ton of confusion. In Episode 10 children learn letter names after becoming confident readers.

Why not start with the letter shapes and then add the sounds?
Starting with what children already know is most effective in teaching. Because children know how to speak, the letter sounds are familiar. Once children have practiced hearing and pronouncing individual letter sounds, they then learn the letter shape for each sound.

Why use sound movements?
The Open Reading sound movements are powerful memory hooks for each letter shape and sound. Since children are inherently physical, these sound movements help children remember the sound and control their voice when sounding out or spelling words.

Why do finger sliding?
Sliding a finger along text helps children's eyes relax as they practice each letter's most common sound.

Note: On some pages, there are arrows under letters and words to help children keep the letters upright, and not turn the card or page upside down by mistake.

Stretch and Snap

Adult says the word if, in, or on.

Child stretches out the word in slow motion, then snaps it back, fast. Next, play with the words fin, sun, mom, ran.

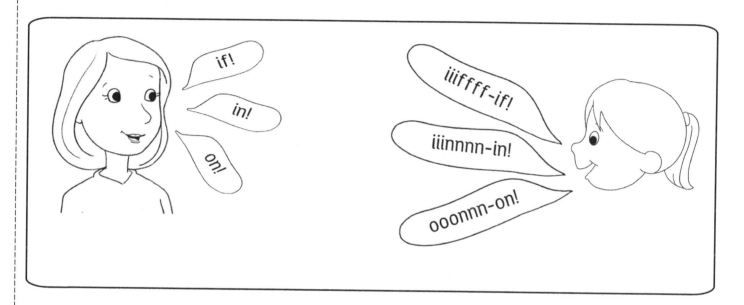

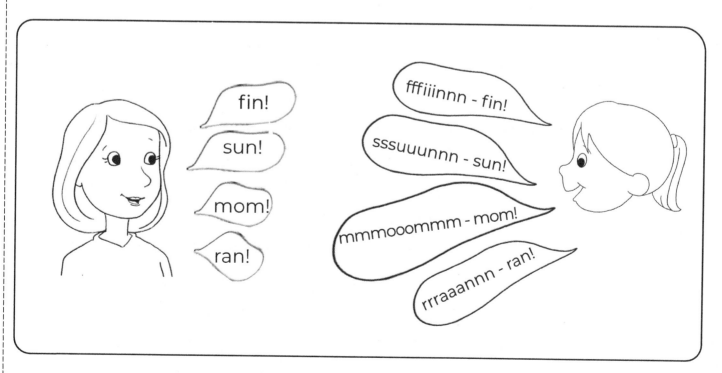

11

Blank Page

Match Game: Letters & Sound Movements

|  Do the sounds and sound movements for each letter. | Cut out the sound movement pictures. Do each sound movement. |  Glue the sound movements under the correct letter shapes. |

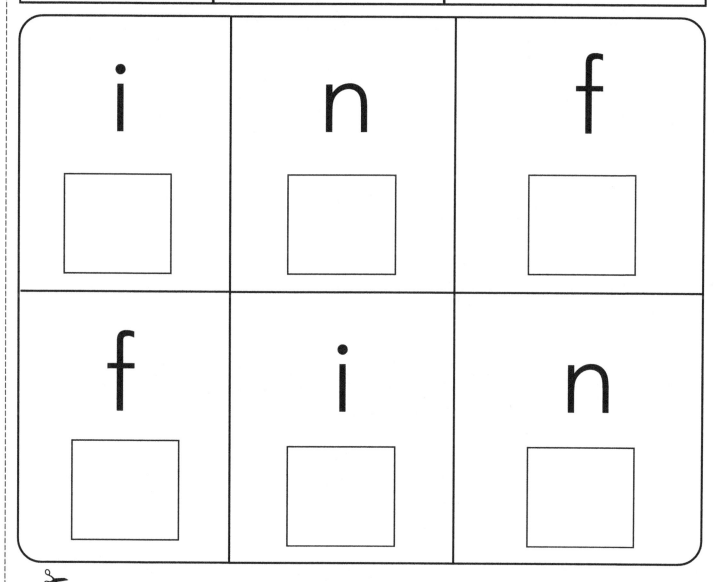

Episode 1/Game 2

Blank Page

Read My Hands

 (f, n, i)

Player 1 silently makes the sound movement for one letter.

Player 2 copies the movement, adds the sound and points to or colors the fish with the correct letter. Then Player 1 makes another movement.

15

Episode 1/Game 3

Blank Page

Sound Bucket - First Sounds

Use a bucket and a ball for each set. Set 1: Cut out then place the **n** card in front of a bucket.	Adult tosses the ball to child and says a word from Set 1, making the *first* sound long and loud.	Child repeats the word with sound movements to figure out the *first* letter sound.	Child throws the ball in the bucket if the word starts with the sound **n**. If not, child throws the ball back to the adult.

Play each set until child is familiar with the first sounds. Then play with the next set.

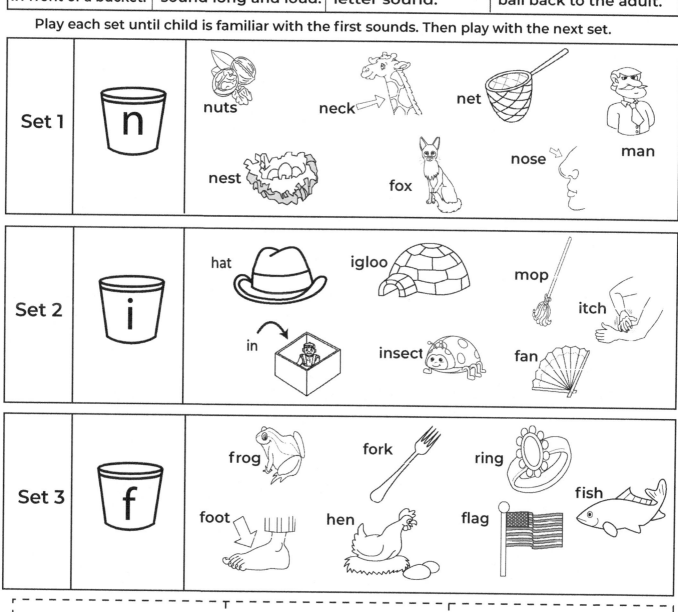

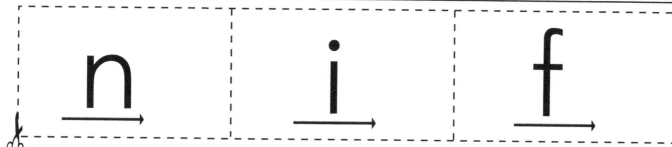

Episode 1/Game 4

Blank Page

Body Letter Shapes

 **Open** Reading

 iii

Make the sound and movement for each letter.

 iii

Then make your body into the letter shape and say its letter sound.

i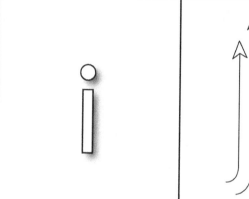

f

n

Episode 1/Game 5

Blank Page

Letter Puzzles

 Cut out all letter pieces and mix them up.	 Child sets the pieces on the letter patterns. Describe each letter piece and then each letter.	 Build the letters without the patterns. Make the sounds and sound movements.

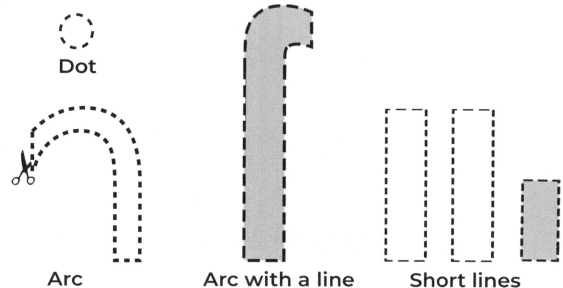

Dot

Arc

Arc with a line

Short lines

21

Blank Page

Slam

 Cut out then spread out the letter cards face up. Player 1 makes the sound and sound movement for a letter.

 Player 2 slams their hands over the matching letter cards before Player 1 counts to three. Player 2 can then try to slam the cards.

i →	n →	f →
i →	n →	f →
i →	n →	f →

Episode 1/Game 7

Blank Page

Find the Hidden Picture

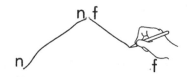

Connect the letters that make the same sound to find the hidden picture.
Do the sounds and sound movements. Color the picture when you are done.

Episode 1/Game 8

Blank Page

Finger Slide

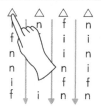

Player 1 places their finger on a triangle and slides down the letters for Player 2.

Player 2 follows the finger with their eyes and says the letter sound and does the movement for each letter.

△	△	△	△
i	n	f	n
f	f	i	i
n	i	i	n
n	n	n	i
i	i	f	f
f	i	n	n

Episode 1/Game 9

Blank Page

Episode 2: Fletcher's Birthday

Overview

Children learn the lowercase letter shapes, sounds, and sound movements for three more letters. They learn to "stretch out" words by saying them in slow motion, identify the "first" and "last" sound in a word and "action spell" words using sound movements.

Episode 2: Pockets, Meg, and friends prepare a surprise birthday for Fletcher.

Quick Tip: Children need to watch each episode over and over. Repeat each episode until they have mastered the skills in that episode before moving onto the next one

Reading Skills

- Use sound movements to connect each letter's common sound to its lowercase shape for *a, m,* and *o.*
- Distinguish between similar letter sounds and shapes: *o,* and *a; m* and *n.*
- "Action spell" words using continuous sound movements and sounds to blend sounds into words without letter shapes.
- Learn the meaning of the word "last" for learning to read.

Open video

Sound Guide

a	-	<u>a</u>t
b	-	ro<u>b</u>
c	-	ki<u>ck</u>
d	-	o<u>dd</u>
e	-	<u>e</u>xit
f	-	o<u>ff</u>
g	-	<u>g</u>o<u>g</u>
h	-	<u>h</u>ot
i	-	<u>i</u>t
j	-	e<u>dge</u>
k	-	ki<u>ck</u>
ck	-	ki<u>ck</u>
l	-	hi<u>ll</u>
m	-	a<u>m</u>
n	-	o<u>n</u>
o	-	<u>o</u>ff
p	-	u<u>p</u>
qu	-	<u>qu</u>it
r	-	<u>h</u>ai<u>r</u>
s	-	u<u>s</u>
t	-	i<u>t</u>
u	-	<u>u</u>p
v	-	lo<u>v</u>e
w	-	o<u>w</u>e
x	-	o<u>x</u>
y	-	happ<u>y</u>
z	-	bu<u>zz</u>
th	-	<u>th</u>is

New letter shapes, sounds, and sound movements

a <u>a</u>t

m a<u>m</u>

o <u>o</u>ff

Episode 2: Fletcher's Birthday

	Games to Play	**Shown in Episode**
1	Sound Buckets - First Sounds	Ep. 2: Part 3
2	Match Game: Letters & Sound Movements	Ep.3: Part 3
3	Read My Hands	Ep. 5: Part 2
4	Letter Puzzles	Ep. 2: Part 2
5	Letter Puzzles	Ep. 2: Part 2
6	Slam	Ep. 2: Part 2
7	Touch and Say	Ep. 2: Part 2
8	Picture Sort	not shown
9	Finger Slide	Ep. 2: Part 2
10	Find the Hidden Picture	not shown
11	Letter/Picture Match	not shown

Tips

Why teach the letters *i, n, f, o, m,* and *a* before other letters?
Of the whole alphabet, these "stretchy letter" sounds can easily be held without distortion.
Also, they are the easiest common sounds for children to blend into two-letter words.

Why start with the short-vowel sounds and not letter names?
The short vowel sound is the most common sound vowels make, and they blend easily
with consonants to make simple two- and three-letter words. Learning the letter names, or long
vowel sounds, before short-vowel sounds can confuse children when first learning to read.

Why hold out letter sounds for different lengths of time?
To pronounce sounds accurately, learn to hold each letter sound for varying lengths of time.

Why name the pictures holding out the first sound?
This helps children isolate the first sound in words and then match that sound to the letter
shape.

How do we "action spell?"
After children hear a word they say the word slowly stretching it out while adding the sound
movements without breaking up the word.

Sound Buckets - First or Last Sound

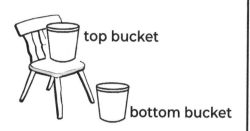 top bucket

bottom bucket

Use two buckets and a ball. Place one higher than the other.
Adult says, "The top bucket is for the 'first' letter sound in a word. The bottom bucket is for the 'last' letter sound in the word."

 ooonnn

Adult stretches out the word *on*. Then asks, "Is the 'nnn' sound the 'first' sound or the 'last' sound in the word *on*?"

 Nnn is the last sound.

Child repeats the word *on* with sound movements then says, "The *nnn* is the 'last' letter sound." Child throws the ball into the bottom bucket.

Note to Adult: Play with words below, asking for the "first" letter sound or the "last" letter sound.
Play often until child is familiar with identifying the "first" and "last" sounds in a word.

Game 1	Say to child: on : Is the nnn sound the "first" or "last" sound in the word *on*? am: is the aaa sound the "first" or "last" sound in the word *am*? in: Is the iii sound the "first" or "last" sound in the word *in*? an: Is the nnn sound the "first" or "last" sound in the word *an*? if: Is the fff sound the "first" or "last" sound in the word *if*?
Game 2	Say to child: an : Is the aaa sound the "first" or "last" sound in the word *an*? on: is the ooo sound the "first" or "last" sound in the word *on*? if: Is the iii sound the "first" or "last" sound in the word *if*? am: Is the mmm sound the "first" or "last" sound in the word *am*? in: Is the nnn sound the "first" or "last" sound in the word *in*?

Episode 2/Game 1

Blank Page

Match Game: Letters & Sound Movements

Do the sound and sound movement for each letter.

Cut out the sound movement pictures. Do each sound movement.

Glue the sound movements under the correct letter shapes.

o

m

a

a

o

m

Episode 2/Game 2

Blank Page

Read My Hands

(i, f, n, o, m, a)

Player 1 silently makes the sound movement for one letter.

Player 2 copies the movement, adds the sound and points to or colors the fish with the correct letter. Then Player 1 makes another movement.

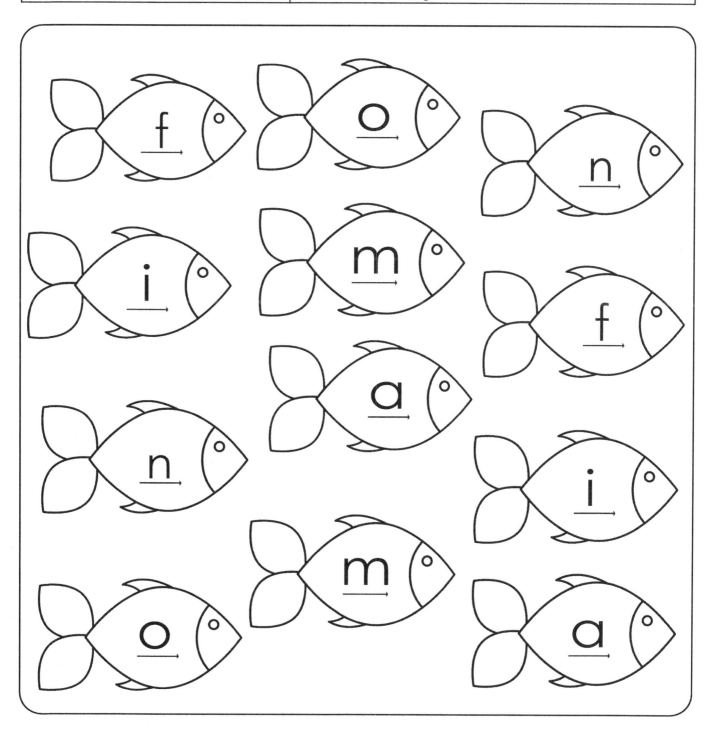

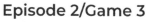

Blank Page

Letter Puzzles

 **Open** Reading

Cut out all letter pieces and mix them up.

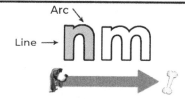
Set the pieces on the letter patterns. Describe each letter piece and then each letter.

Build the letters without the patterns. Make the sounds and sound movements.

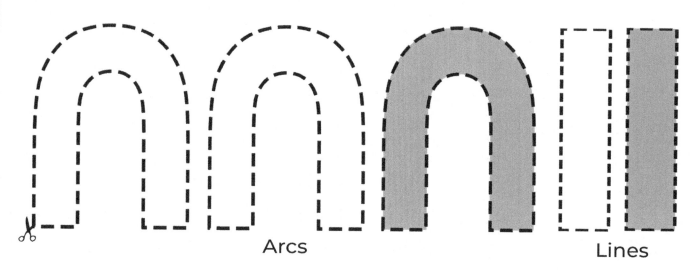

Arcs

Lines

Episode 2/Game 4

Blank Page

Letter Puzzles

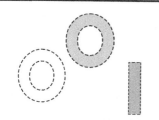
Cut out all letter pieces and mix them up.

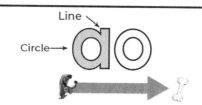
Set the pieces on the letter patterns. Describe each letter piece and then each letter.

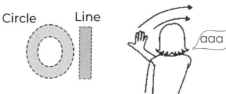
Build the letters without the patterns. Make the sounds and sound movements.

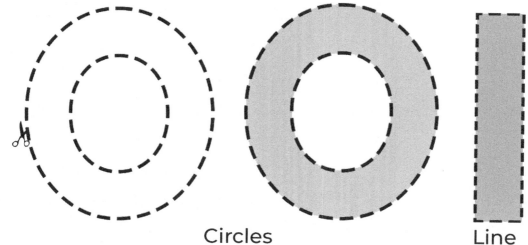

Circles   Line

Episode 2/Game 5

Blank Page

Slam

Cut out then spread out the letter cards face up. Player 1 makes the sound and sound movement for a letter.

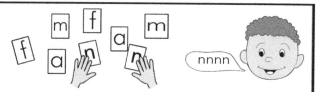

Player 2 slams their hands over the matching letter cards before Player 1 counts to three. Player 2 can then try to slam the cards.

i →	o →	a →
m →	a →	i →
f →	m →	o →
n →	f →	n →

Episode 2/Game 6

Blank Page

Touch and Say

Player 1 silently holds their finger on a letter for varying lengths of time.

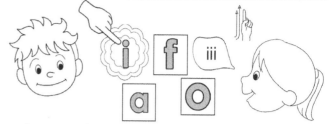

Player 2 does the sound and movement as long as Player 1 is touching the letter.

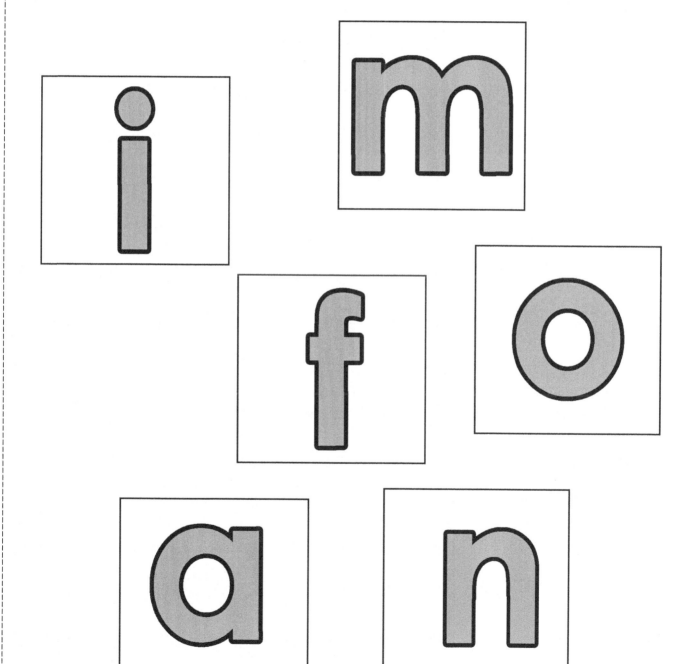

Episode 2/Game 7

Blank Page

Picture Sort

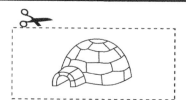

Cut out the picture cards. Say each word. Do the sound and movement for the first sound.

Glue the pictures under the letter that is the first sound in the word.

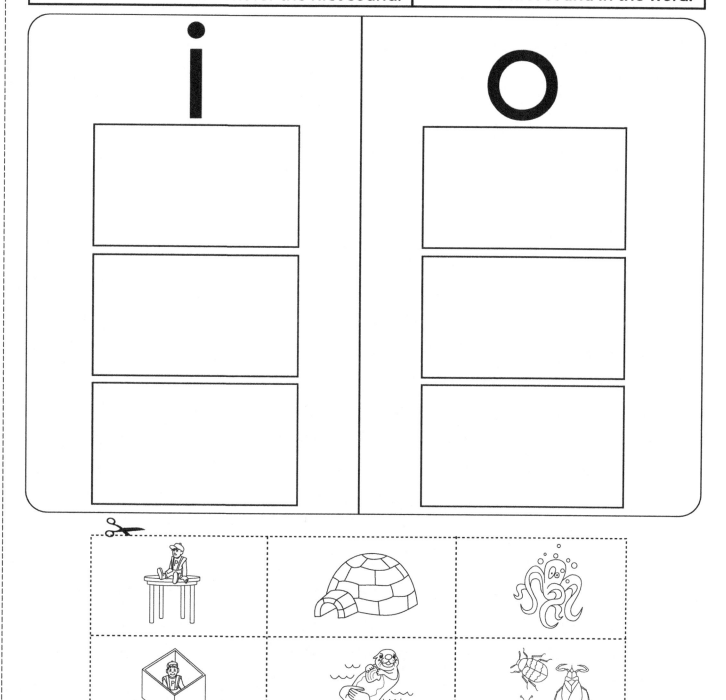

Episode 2/Game 8

Blank Page

Finger Slide

Player 1 places their finger on a triangle and slides down the letters for Player 2.

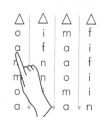 

Player 2 follows the finger with their eyes and says the letter sound and does the movement for each letter.

△	△	△	△
o	i	m	f
a	f	a	i
m	n	a	f
o	i	o	i
a	f	a	n

Episode 2/Game 9

Blank Page

Find the Hidden Picture

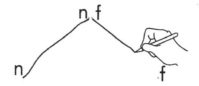

Connect the letters that make the same sound to find the hidden picture.
Do the sounds and sound movements. Color the picture when you are done.

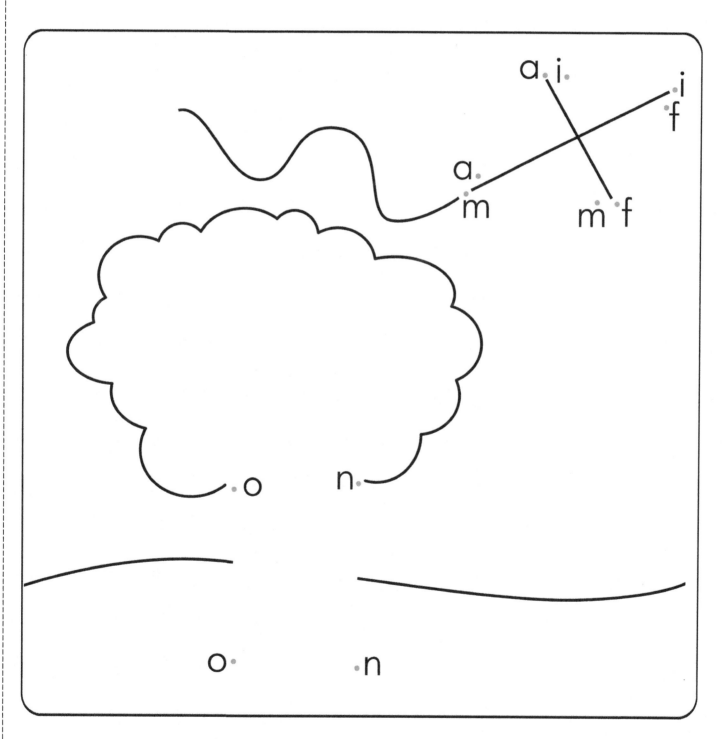

Episode 2/Game 10

Blank Page

Letter/Picture Match

Do the letter sounds and sound movements.
Draw a line connecting the letter to the picture that starts with the letter sound.

o

m

a

Episode 2/Game 11

Blank Page

Episode 3: Fletcher's Circus

Overview

Children learn to blend letter sounds to make two-letter words, look ahead when reading, spell words using sound movements and understand how to hold and read a book. They read treasure hunt clues and the first of the <u>Little Book</u> series.

Episode 3: Pockets, Fletcher, and friends create a circus and sound out two-letter words.

Quick Tip: For most children, watching a whole episode in one sitting is not going to be an effective way to learn. Instead, have them watch just a part of the episode at a time. Repeat each part as many times as they like as they play their way through this Game Book.

Reading Skills

- Review letters *i, n, f, o, m,* and *a*.
- Slide the pointer finger to move eyes along letters for tracking text with ease.
- Look from "first" to "last" letter to smoothly slide sounds together to read a word.
- Read treasure hunt clues to draw conclusions about where to find the next clues and the treasure.
- Learn about book format, cover, and title page. Then read the first <u>Little Book</u> by reading the words and making up a story to go with the pictures.

Open video

Sound Guide

a	-	<u>a</u>t
b	-	ro<u>b</u>
c	-	ki<u>ck</u>
d	-	o<u>dd</u>
e	-	<u>e</u>xit
f	-	o<u>ff</u>
g	-	fo<u>g</u>
h	-	<u>h</u>ot
i	-	<u>i</u>t
j	-	e<u>dge</u>
k	-	ki<u>ck</u>
ck	-	ki<u>ck</u>
l	-	hi<u>ll</u>
m	-	a<u>m</u>
n	-	o<u>n</u>
o	-	<u>o</u>ff
p	-	u<u>p</u>
qu	-	<u>qu</u>it
r	-	hai<u>r</u>
s	-	u<u>s</u>
t	-	i<u>t</u>
u	-	<u>u</u>p
v	-	lo<u>v</u>e
w	-	o<u>w</u>e
x	-	o<u>x</u>
y	-	happ<u>y</u>
z	-	bu<u>zz</u>
th	-	<u>th</u>is

Review letter shapes, sounds, and sound movements

i <u>i</u>n   **f** o<u>ff</u>   **n** o<u>n</u>

o <u>o</u>ff   **m** a<u>m</u>   **a** <u>a</u>t

Episode 3: Fletcher's Circus

	Games to Play	Shown in Episode
1	Eye Tracking	Ep. 1: Part 3
2	Letter/Sound Movement Match	not shown
3	Picture Sort	not shown
4	Sound Buckets - First Sounds	Ep. 2: Part 3
5	Letter Hunt	not shown
6	Find the Hidden Picture	not shown
7	Match Game: in, on	Ep. 3: Part 3
8	Treasure Hunt	Ep. 6: Part 3
9	Little Book: Fletcher Finds Pockets	Ep. 3: Part 3

Tips

Why teach blending two-letter words top down?
Teaching one skill at a time is good teaching practice. Therefore to read a word children first learn to blend two sounds together in the *easy* top-down direction. In Episode 4 they learn to use the more challenging left-to-right direction.

Why put letters beside all sorts of other shapes?
This helps children distinguish between the shapes of letters and other distracting shapes.

Why do the first Little Books have only a few words?
By combining just one or two words with a picture, children get to invent a storyline while enjoying satisfaction of reading the whole book.

Why do treasure hunts?
Treasure hunts are a terrific way to channel the nervous, excited energy of beginning readers. Clues challenge children to use critical thinking and problem solving as they read instead of using rote memory. They get to run from one hiding spot to another, following the clues until they find the treasure. What better way to incentivize children to start reading!

Eye Tracking

Trace the trail with your finger, connecting the two pictures that go together.

Then use a pencil or crayon to trace the trail.

Episode 3/Game 1

Blank Page

Letter/Sound Movement Match

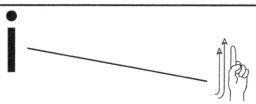

Do the sounds and sound movements.
Draw a line connecting the letter to the correct sound movement.

i

m

f

o

n

a

Episode 3/Game 2

Blank Page

Picture Sort

Cut out the pictures. Stretch out the words. Then do the sound and movement for the first sound in each word.

Glue the pictures under the letter for the first sound in the word.

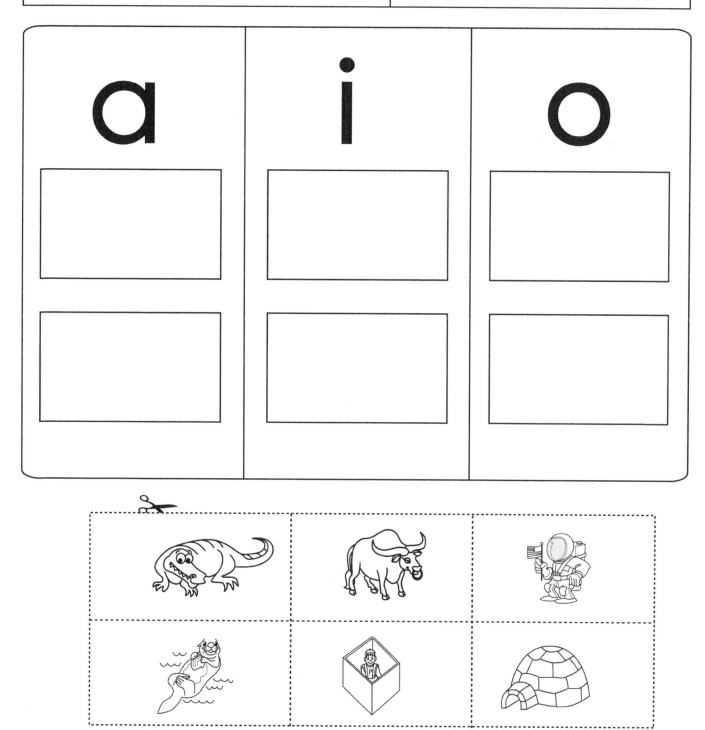

Episode 3/Game 3

Blank Page

Sound Buckets - First Sounds

 Use two buckets and a ball. **Set 1:** Cut out then place the cards **n** and **m** in front of the buckets.	 Adult says a word from Set 1, making the *first* sound long and loud.	 To figure out the *first* letter, child repeats the word, and makes the sound movement for the first sound.	 Child throws the ball in the correct bucket.

Play each set until child is familiar with the *first* sounds. Then play with the next set.

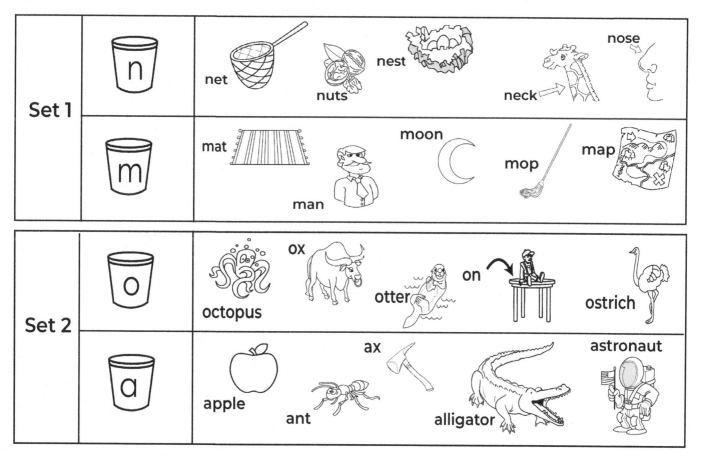

Set 1
- n — net, nuts, nest, neck, nose
- m — mat, man, moon, mop, map

Set 2
- o — octopus, ox, otter, on, ostrich
- a — apple, ant, ax, alligator, astronaut

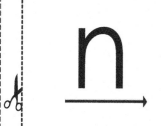 

n   m   o   a

Episode 3/Game 4

Blank Page

Letter Hunt

f n^a o i m Find the letters hidden in and around the castle.	 Circle the letters as you find them. Do the sounds and movements.

63

Blank Page

Find the Hidden Picture

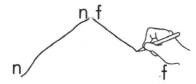

Connect the letters that make the same sound to find the hidden picture.
Do the sounds and sound movements. Color the picture when you are done.

m a

i
n

i
o

m o

n a

Episode 3/Game 6

Blank Page

Match Game: in, on

Open Reading

Discuss the pictures using the words *on* or *in*.

Cut out the word cards. To read each word, stretch out the sounds and do the sound movements. Clap each word 3 times and use it in a sentence.

Glue the word cards under the correct picture.

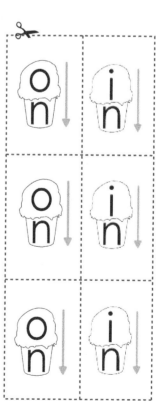

Episode 3 Game 7

Blank Page

Treasure Hunt

 **Open** Reading

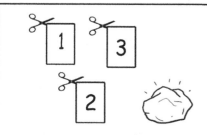

Cut out clue cards.
To make a treasure, wrap a snack, coin or small toy in aluminum foil.

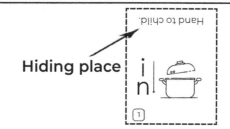

Hiding place

Hand to child.

Hiding places are upside down on clue cards.
Before the hunt, without the child, hide clues and treasure.

Hand clue 1 to the child. Give hints during the hunt if needed. Have fun!

Hand this clue to child.

1

Hide this clue in a large pot.

2

Hide this clue on a table or desk.

3

Hide treasure in a jacket pocket.

Episode 3 Game 8

Blank Page

Fletcher Finds Pockets

OpenReading
Episode 3

Episode 3: Fletcher Finds Pockets

Vocabulary List

Before reading this book, review the two words below. Make several of each word card on slips of paper so child can hop along a reading Word Trail. Play the Word Trail the same as a Sound Trail.

Remember: Children already understand the top-down direction so write the 2-letter words top-down.

Use this skill to learn to blend two sounds to read a word, and then learn the left-to-right reading direction.

Book Vocabulary Words

o
n

i
n

o
n

(2)

Make the book
1. To keep the pages in story order, cut the pages from the game book as a group.

2. Cut the pile of pages along the two cut lines.

3. Remove this page and the vocabulary page from the top of the piles.

4. Begin the book with the cover pile. Then put the next 3 piles below each other following the page numbers.

5. Staple the book along the left side.

Read the book
Have child slide their finger down the arrow next to the words as they blend sounds and movements to read the words.

Child uses the words and pictures to make up a story.

Blank Page

Episode 3

Fletcher Finds Pockets

A Fletcher's Place
Little Book

Colored by:

_____

Story by Irene Hamaker
Illustrated by Matt Beraz
Layout by Cyndy Lemyre

5

3

7

Blank Page

Blank Page

Episode 4: The Skateboard Jump

Open Reading

Overview

Children learn lowercase letter shapes, sounds and sound movements for four more letters. They learn the left-to-right reading direction and begin reading three-letter words.

Episode 4: Fletcher builds a skateboard jump and skates down the ramp.

[QR code] **Open video**

Reading Skills

- Use sound movements to connect each letter's common sound to its lowercase shape for *l, u, j,* and *s*.
- Learn the left-right-reading direction.
- Sound out and spell three-letter words.
- Look ahead at all letters before reading a word.
- Read treasure hunt clues to draw conclusions about where to find the next clues and the treasure.
- Read the <u>Little Book</u> by reading words and making up the story to go with the pictures.

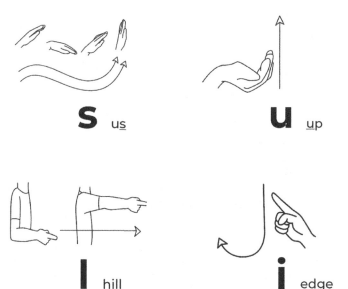

New letter shapes, sounds, and sound movements

s u<u>s</u>

u <u>u</u>p

l hi<u>ll</u>

j e<u>dge</u>

Sound Guide

a	-	<u>a</u>t
b	-	ro<u>b</u>
c	-	ki<u>ck</u>
d	-	o<u>dd</u>
e	-	<u>e</u>xit
f	-	o<u>ff</u>
g	-	fo<u>g</u>
h	-	<u>h</u>ot
i	-	<u>i</u>t
j	-	e<u>dge</u>
k	-	ki<u>ck</u>
ck	-	ki<u>ck</u>
l	-	hi<u>ll</u>
m	-	a<u>m</u>
n	-	o<u>n</u>
o	-	<u>o</u>ff
p	-	u<u>p</u>
qu	-	<u>qu</u>it
r	-	hai<u>r</u>
s	-	u<u>s</u>
t	-	i<u>t</u>
u	-	<u>u</u>p
v	-	lo<u>v</u>e
w	-	o<u>w</u>e
x	-	o<u>x</u>
y	-	happ<u>y</u>
z	-	bu<u>zz</u>
th	-	<u>th</u>is

Note: You will find reading arrows on page 7, and on page 401. Use them for reading games. Place them below letters, phrases, words and sentences as you read together.

Episode 4: The Skateboard Jump

Words children can now read:

Words that are two- or three-letters long:

Words with *u* first or in the middle: **us, fun, sun, mum.**

Words with *a* in the middle: **fan, man, jam.**

Words with *i* in the middle: **fin, sis.**

Word with *o* in the middle: **mom.**

	Games to Play	Shown in Episode
1	Read My Hands	Ep. 5: Part 2
2	Match Game: Letters & Sound Movements	Ep. 3: Part 3
3	Letter Puzzles	Ep. 4: Part 1
4	Letter Puzzles	Ep. 4: Part 1
5	Letter Puzzles	Ep. 4: Part 1
6	Sound Trail	Ep. 4: Part 1
7	Sound Maze	Ep. 4: Part 1
8	Slam	Ep. 2: Part 2
9	The Reading Direction	Ep. 4: Part 2
10	Finger Sliding Animal Sounds	Ep. 4: Part 2
11	The Ice Cream Vowels	not shown
12	Ice Cream & Cookie Sounds	Ep. 4: Part 3
13	Word Builder	Ep. 4: Part 3
14	Sound Run	Ep. 4: Part 3
15	Treasure Hunt	Ep. 6: Part 3
16	Little Book: Fletcher's Present	Ep. 4: Part 3

Tips

Why run while sliding sounds together or jump on letters and words instead of drilling with flashcards?
Running to slide sounds together to blend sounds into words makes reading child's play. Jumping while looking at letter or word cards on the floor makes learning exciting.

Why use the Fletcher's Place left-to-right reading arrow?
Mastering the left-to-right reading direction is a key skill for beginning readers. Have children place this arrow under any words or texts they are reading. When reading other books to children, model using the arrow by placing it below the sentences as you read.

Why have children finger slide?
Finger sliding under words trains the eyes to relax, directs children to look at letters in left to right reading order, and look ahead.

Why recall a sequence of animal sounds instead of letter sounds that make a word?
Children already know animal sounds so they first practice holding a series of animal sounds in their mind and then repeating them from memory. Then they transition this skill to remembering and saying a series of two and then three letter sounds from memory.

Why refer to vowels as "ice-cream sounds," consonants as "cookie sounds," and three-letter words as "ice-cream sandwiches?"
At first, Fletcher's Place uses language children already understand and remember. Later episodes add the more technical terms and eventually drop the user-friendly terms. For example, consonants are first called "cookie sounds" then "cookie-consonants" and finally consonants.

Read My Hands

 (s, u, l, j, a)

Player 1 silently makes the sound movement for one letter.

Player 2 copies the movement, adds the sound and points to or colors the fish with the correct letter. Then Player 1 makes another movement.

Episode 4/Game 1

Blank Page

Match Game: Letters & Sound Movements

Open Reading

Do the sounds and sound movements for each letter.

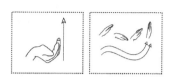

Cut out the sound movement pictures. Do each sound movement.

Glue the sound movements next to the correct letter shapes.

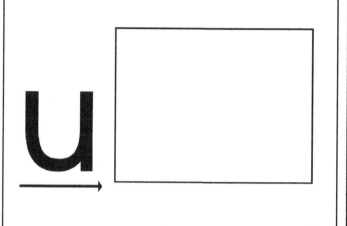

u

s

l

j

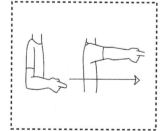

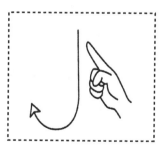

81

Episode 4/Game 2

Blank Page

Letter Puzzles

Cut out letter pieces and mix them up.

Set the pieces on the letter patterns. Describe each letter piece and then each letter.

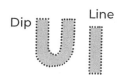

Build the letters without the patterns. Make the sounds and sound movements.

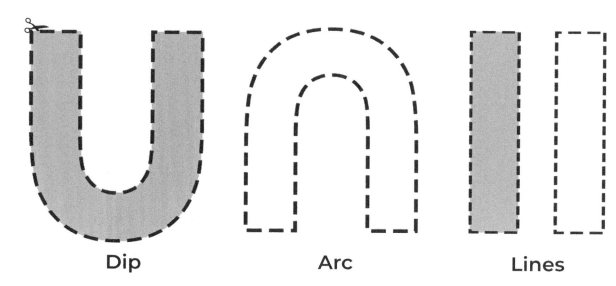

Dip   Arc   Lines

83

Episode 4/Game 3

Blank Page

Letter Puzzles

Cut out letter pieces and mix them up.

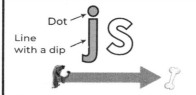

Set the pieces on the letter patterns. Describe each letter piece and then each letter.

Build the letters without the patterns. Make the sounds and sound movements.

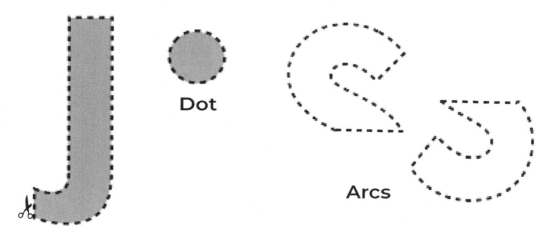

Line with a dip

Dot

Arcs

Episode 4/Game 4

Blank Page

Letter Puzzles

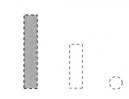

Cut out letter pieces and mix them up.

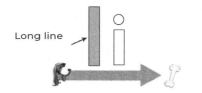

Long line

Set the pieces on the letter patterns. Describe each letter piece and then each letter.

Long line

Build the letters without the patterns. Make the sounds and sound movements.

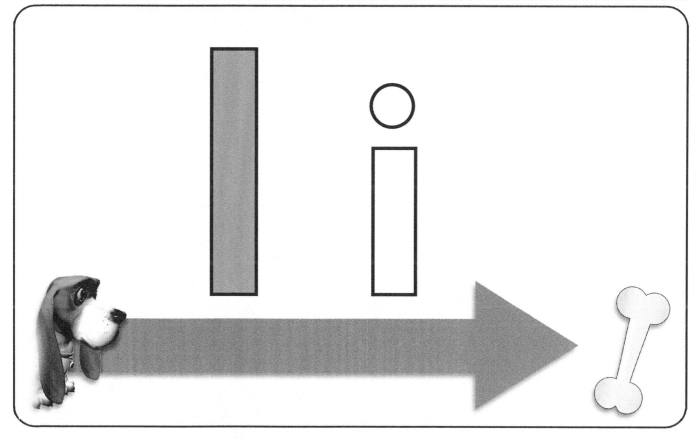

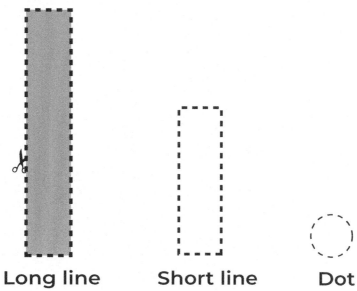

Long line **Short line** **Dot**

Episode 4/Game 5

Blank Page

Sound Trail

Cut out the cards.
Set them in a trail on the floor.

Jump on each card while making the sound and sound movement.

u →	u →	s →	s →
l →	l →	j →	j →
a →	a →	o →	o →
m →	m →	n →	n →

Episode 4/Game 6

Blank Page

Sound Maze

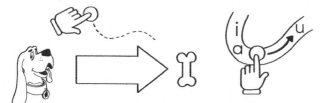

Finger slide from Fletcher the dog **to the bone.**

At the same time, do the sounds and sound movements.

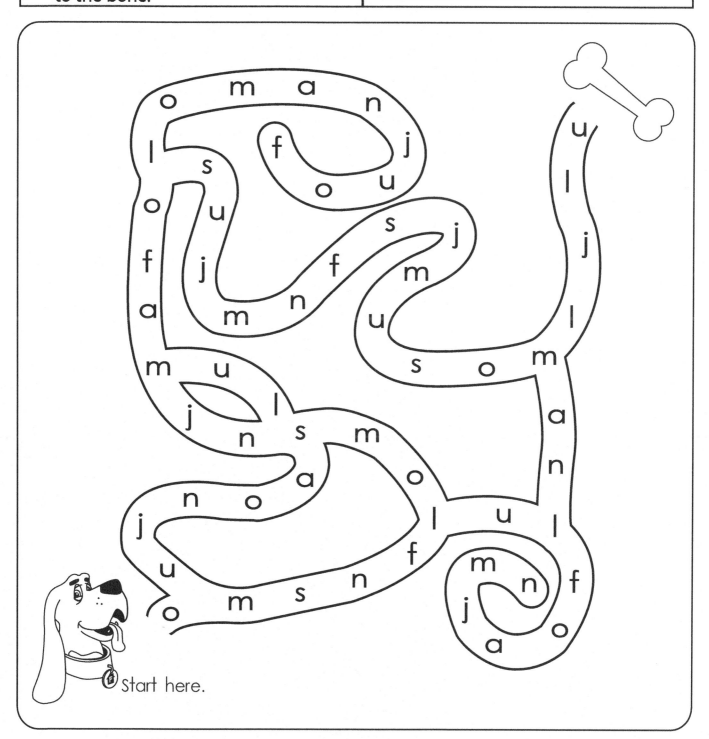

Start here.

91   Episode 4/Game 7

Blank Page

Slam

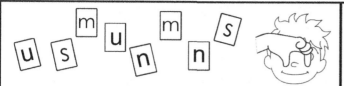

Cut out then spread out the letter cards face up. Player 1 makes the sound and sound movement for a letter.

Player 2 slams their hands over the matching letter cards before Player 1 counts to three. Player 2 can then try to slam the cards.

a →	a →	u →	u →
s →	s →	l →	l →
m →	m →	o →	o →
n →	n →	j →	j →

Episode 4/Game 8

Blank Page

The Reading Direction

We read from left to right.
Roll up your left sleeve.
Touch your left knee.

Slide your finger along the arrow from the dog to the bone. Say the objects you see in a row on the table, ceiling, and floor.

Jar, lid, salt.

"Read" objects in a row on a table.

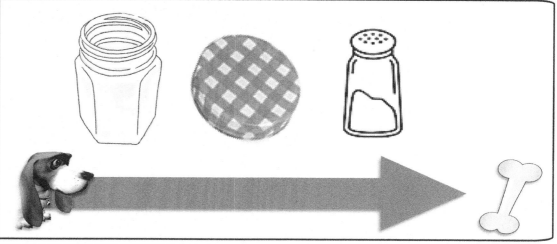

"Read" objects on the ceiling.

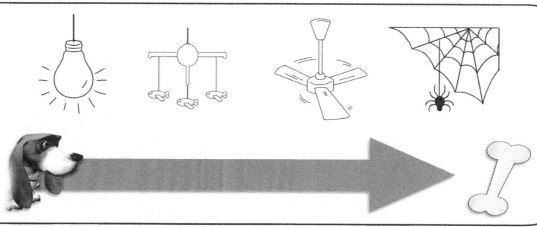

"Read" objects on the floor.

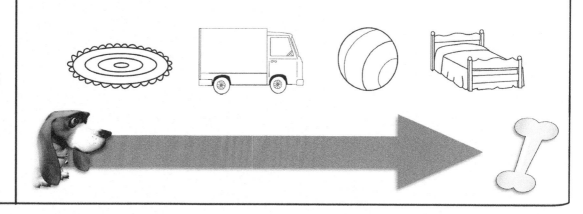

Episode 4/Game 9

Blank Page

Finger Sliding Animal Sounds

Cut out cards. Place 2, 3, or 4 animal cards along the arrow. Player 1 slides their finger under the cards and says the animal sounds.

Player 2 covers the cards. Player 1 says the animal sounds in reading order from memory. Discuss different ways to remember the sounds in order.

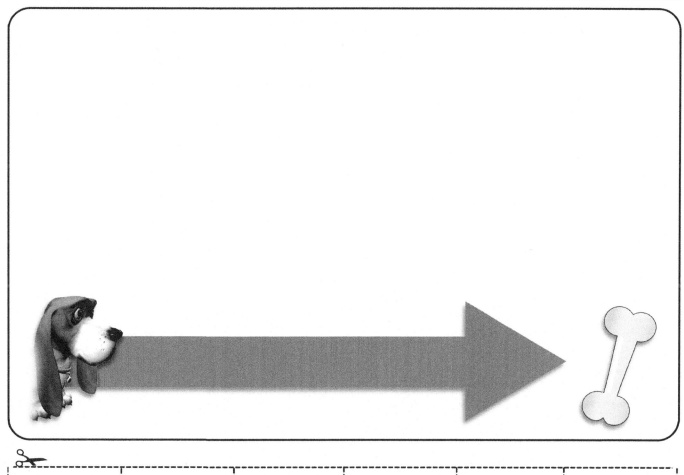

Episode 4/Game 10

Blank Page

Find the Ice-Cream Vowels

Open
Reading

Look for these ice-cream vowels.
Do their sounds and sound movements.

Color all the balloons that have
ice-cream vowels in them.

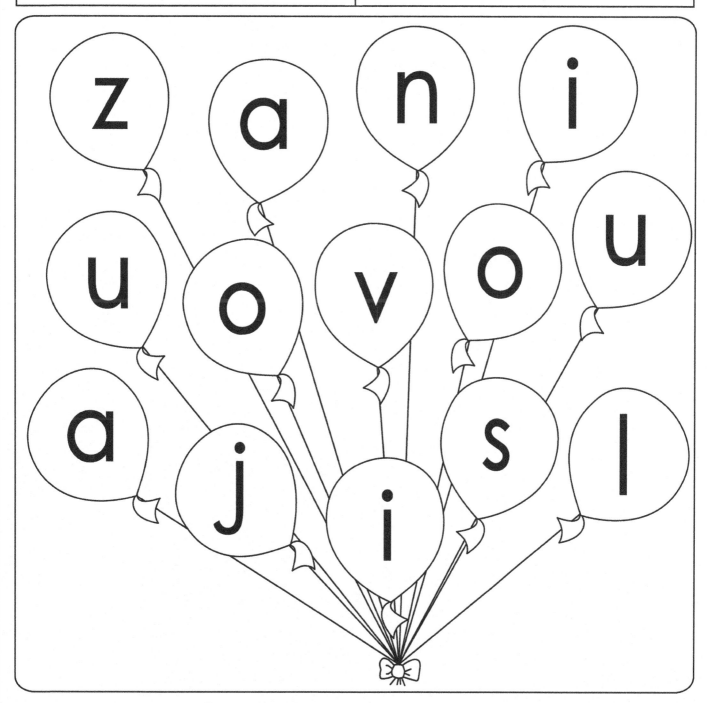

Episode 4/Game 11

Blank Page

Ice-Cream & Cookie Sounds

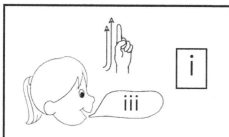

Cut out the letters and do the sounds and movements.

Open your mouth to say ice-cream vowel sounds. Bite down on cookie-consonant sounds.

Put ice-cream letters on the ice creams (a, i, o) and the cookie letters on the cookies (n, f, m).

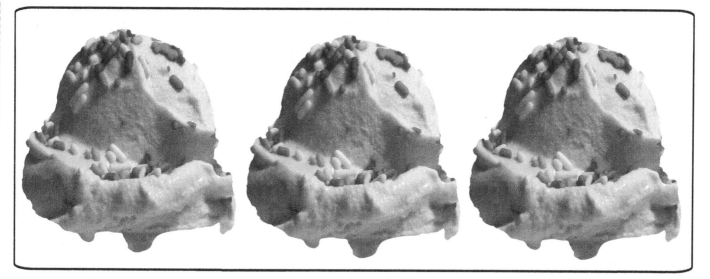

f n o i m a

Episode 4/Game 12

Blank Page

Word Builder

  Cut out the letter cards. Child places the ice-cream vowels on the ice cream and the cookie consonants on the cookie. Do the sounds and movements.

 Adult says the word "sun." Child stretches out the word and does the sounds and movements.

 Child places the letters on the word builder to spell the word sun. Child checks spelling with sounds and movements.

Next, do the steps for the words fun, fan, fin.

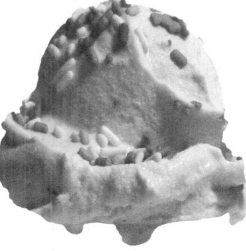

u
a
i

s
n
f

Episode 4/Game 13

Blank Page

Sound Run

Play with two sounds first.
Cut out the cards for the words *if* and *us*.

Child takes the *i* letter and reads the sound as they run to the adult with the *f* letter. Child adds the last sound, *f*, to say the word *if*. Have child use the word in a sentence. Now, play with the letters *u* and *s* to make the word *us*.

i	f	u	s

Play with three sounds. Cut out the cards for the words *sun*, *jam* and *man*.

Child slides two sounds, *su*, together and says the *u* sound as they run to the adult with the *n*.

suunnn
Sun! Sun! Sun!
The sun is hot.

Child adds the last sound to read *sun* and says a sentence. Now play with the cards for the words *jam*, and *man*.

su	n
ja	m
ma	n

Blank Page

Treasure Hunt

 **Open** Reading

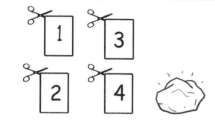

Cut out clue cards. To make a treasure, wrap a snack, coin or small toy in aluminum foil.

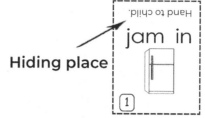

Hiding place

Hiding places are upside down on clue cards. Before the hunt, without the child, hide the clues and treasure.

Hand a reading arrow and clue 1 to the child. Give hints during hunt if needed. Have fun!

Hand this clue to child.

jam in

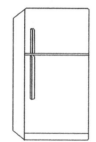

1

Hide this clue in a fridge.

on mom

2

Hide this clue on a mom or picture of a mom.

in

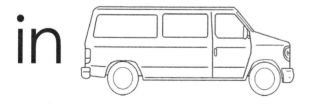

3

Hide this clue in a van or toy van or car.
Hide treasure in an umbrella.

if

4

Episode 4/Game 15

Blank Page

Episode 4

Open Reading

Episode 4: Fletcher's Present

Vocabulary List
Before reading this book, review the list below. Make word cards on slips of paper so child can hop along a Word Trail. Play the Word Trail the same as a Sound Trail.

Book Vocabulary Words

if

in

on

sun

fun

if

3

Make the book
1. To keep the pages in story order, cut the pages from the game book as a group.

2. Then cut the pile of pages along the two cut lines.

3. Remove this page and the vocabulary page from the top of the piles.

4. Begin the book with the cover pile. Then put the next 3 piles below each other following the page numbers.

5. Staple the book along the left side.

Read the book
Have child place a reading arrow below each word and slide their finger along the reading arrow as they read.

Child uses the words and pictures to make up a story.

Blank Page

Episode 4

Fletcher's Present

A Fletcher's Place
Little Book

Colored by:

_____

Story by Irene Hamaker
Illustrated by Matt Beraz
Layout by Cyndy Lemyre

if

7

fun

4

fun

10

Blank Page

if

1

on

8

if

5

Blank Page

sun

2

if

9

in

6

Blank Page

Episode 5: Fletcher Paints

Open Reading

Open video

Overview

Children learn the lowercase letter shapes, sounds, and sound movements for four more letters. They learn that "snap sound" letters don't stretch. They learn to read four-letter words ending in "snap sounds" and double consonants. They read two-word phrases and learn about rhyming words and homonyms.

Episode 5: Fletcher paints a portrait of the friends.

Reading Skills

- Use sound movements to connect each letter's common sound to its lowercase shape for *r, z, v*, and *t*.
- Learn how to pronounce the "snap sound" *t*.
- Sound out and spell three- and four-letter words with twin consonants at the end.
- Learn how to pronounce the irregular word *a*.
- Learn about rhyming words like *sun* and *fun* and homonyms like *fit* meaning "a fit mutt" or "the shirt doesn't fit."
- Call vowels and consonants ice-cream vowels and cookie consonants.
- Read treasure hunt clues to draw conclusions about where to find the next clues and the treasure.
- Read the <u>Little Book</u> by reading the phrases and making up the story to go with the pictures.

New letter shapes, sounds, and sound movements

r hai<u>r</u>

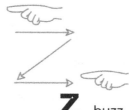

z bu<u>zz</u>

v lo<u>v</u>e

i<u>t</u>

Episode 5: Fletcher Paints

Words children can now read:

Words that begin with *r, v*: **ram, ran, van; rim; run.**

Words that end with *t*: **at, fat, mat, rat, sat, vat; it, fit, lit, sit; jot lot, not, rot; jut, nut, rut.**

Note: Fletcher's Place teaches words beginning with t in Episode 8.

Words that end with "twin" consonants: **mass, jazz; ill, fill, sill, fizz, miss, mitt; off, loss, moss; fuss, fuzz, mutt.**

A word that is a "clown sound" (irregular word): **a.** This word says "uh."

	Games to Play	Shown in Episode
1	Read My Hands	Ep. 5: Part 2
2	Sound Buckets - First Sounds	Ep. 2: Part 3
3	Match Game: Letters & Sound Movements	Ep.3: Part 3
4	Memory	Ep. 5: Part 1
5	Word/Picture Match	not shown
6	Letter Puzzles	Ep. 5: Part 1
7	Letter Puzzles	Ep. 5: Part 1
8	Word/Picture Match	not shown
9	Word Builder	Ep. 5: Part 2
10	Silly Mixed-Up Spelling	Ep. 9: Part 2
11	Word Puzzles	Ep. 5: Part 3
12	Rhyming Words Trail	not shown
13	Phrase/Picture Match	Ep. 5: Part 3
14	Treasure Hunt	Ep. 6: Part 3
15	<u>Little Book: Fletcher Paints Sam</u>	Ep. 5: Part 3

Note: You will find reading arrows on page 7, and on page 401. Use them for reading games. Place them below letters, phrases, words and sentences as you read together.

Tips

How can I help children pronounce the "snap sound" *t* accurately (and later *b, d, c, k, p*, and *g*)?
Say the "snap sounds" quickly with a short burst of air and keep the jaw from dropping. Do not add the "uh" sound after the letter sound.

How can children learn to hear the individual sounds in words if they don't pause between sounds?
Children will be able to hear and count the individual sounds in a word as they stretch out the word, saying it in slow motion as in "sssuuunnn," while adding the corresponding sound movements. In contrast, when children pause between sounds, many have trouble putting the word back together.

Why is the word *a*, a word with a "clown sound" (an irregular word)?
Words with "clown sounds," or irregular words, have letters that don't follow normal English spelling patterns like the letter /o/ in *no, so, go*, or the letter /a/ in *want*.

Students identify the letter within a word that is "clowning around," not saying its normal sound. Recognizing one irregular letter in a word is easier than memorizing a whole word. To remember that this letter is "clowning around," make the "clown sound" movement (one hand on their head) while making the sound movement for the letter with their other hand. When written, a triangle represents a clown hat.

Read My Hands

 (v,r,z,t)

Player 1 silently makes the sound movement for one letter.

Player 2 copies the movement, adds the sound and points to the fish with the correct letter. Then Player 1 makes another movement.

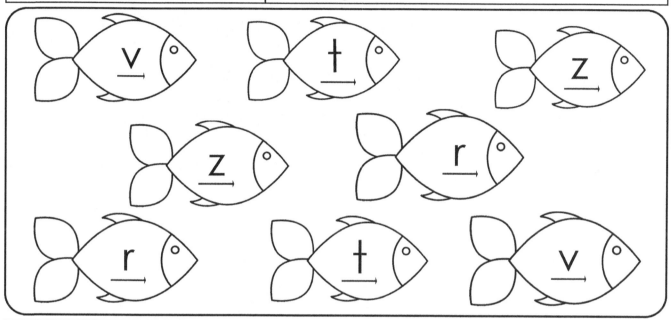

 van

Cut out the cards and place upside down in a pile. Player 1 picks up a card, silently makes the sound movements for a word without showing it to Player 2.

 van

Player 2 does the sound movements with Player 1 and adds the sounds. When Player 2 says the correct word, Player 1 gives the card to Player 2.

van	sat	nut
run	mat	rot

119

Blank Page

Sound Buckets - First Sounds

Open Reading

Use two buckets and a ball for each set.
Set 1: Cut out then place the cards *s* and *z* in front of the buckets.

Adult says a word from Set 1, making the *first* sound long and loud.

To figure out the *first* letter, child repeats the word, and makes the sound movement for the first sound.

Child throws the ball in the correct bucket.

Play each set until child is familiar with the *first* sounds. Then play with the next set.

Set 1

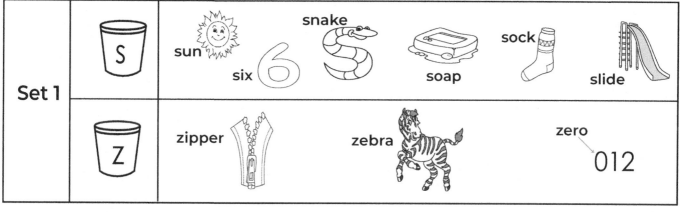

sun, six, snake, soap, sock, slide

zipper, zebra, zero 012

Set 2

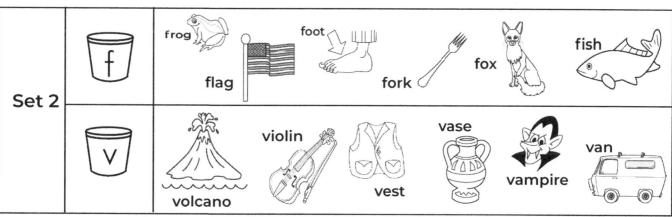

frog, flag, foot, fork, fox, fish

volcano, violin, vest, vase, vampire, van

s →   z →   v →   f →

Episode 5/Game 2

Blank Page

Match Game: Letters & Sound Movements

Do the sounds and sound movements for each letter.	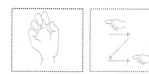 Cut out the sound movement pictures. Do each sound movement.	 Glue the sound movements next to the correct letter shapes.

 r

z

v

t

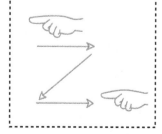

Episode 5/Game 3

Blank Page

Memory

Cut out the cards. Spread them out face down. Player 1 turns up two cards, does the sounds and movements for the letters.

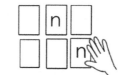

If they match, Player 1 takes the cards.

If cards do not match, place them face down. Then Player 2 takes a turn.

n	r	s	t	u
a	t	o	r	z
z	f	v	f	a
o	s	u	n	v

Episode 5/Game 4

Blank Page

Word/Picture Match

 **on**

Read the words smoothly sliding the sounds and sound movements together without a break.

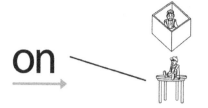 **on**

Draw a line from the word to the correct picture.

on

in

sun

fan

man

jam

Episode 5/Game 5

Blank Page

Letter Puzzles

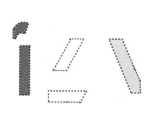

Cut out letter pieces and mix them up.

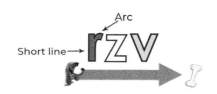

Set the pieces on the letter patterns. Describe each letter piece and then each letter.

Build the letters without the patterns. Make the sounds and sound movements.

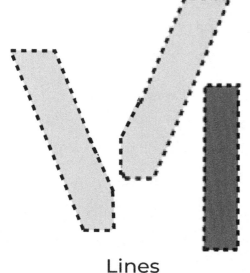

Lines

Arc

Short lines

Episode 5/ Game 6

Blank Page

Letter Puzzles

Cut out letter pieces and mix them up.

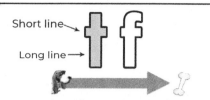

Short line

Long line

Set the pieces on the letter patterns. Describe each letter piece and then each letter.

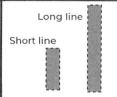

Long line

Short line

Build the letters without the patterns. Make the sounds and sound movements.

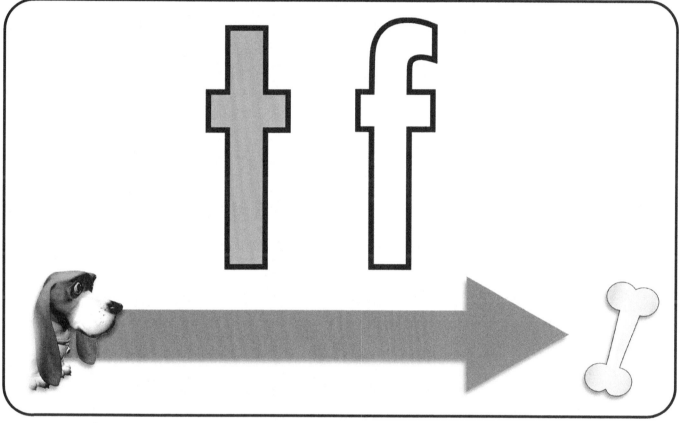

Long line

Arc with a line

Short lines

131

Blank Page

Word/Picture Match

sun
run

Read the words smoothly sliding the sounds and sound movements together without a break.

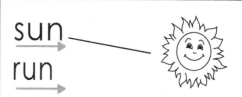

sun
run

Draw a line from the correct word to the picture.

sun

sam

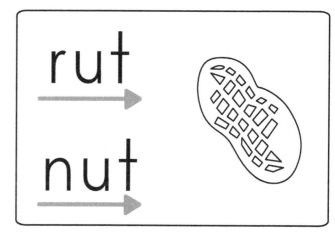

rut

nut

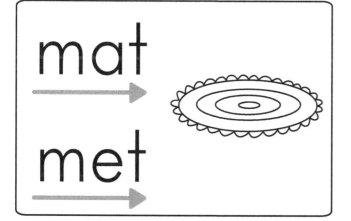

mat

met

jazz

jam

nut

net

fat

fit

Episode 5/Game 8

Blank Page

Word Builder

Cut out the letter cards. Child places the ice-cream vowels on the ice cream and the cookie consonants on the cookie. Do the sounds and movements.

Adult says the word "fit." Child stretches out the word and does the sounds and movements.

Child places the letters on the word builder to spell the word *fit*. Child checks spelling with sounds and movements.

Do the steps for the words fit, sit, sat, fat, rat.

i
a
s

t
r
f

Episode 5/Game 9

Blank Page

Silly Mixed-Up Spelling

Cut out the cards. Point to the letters on the cookie and ice cream. Have child do the sounds and movements.

Adult reads a word from the list below.

Child stretches the word then does the sounds and movements. Next, spells the word by placing letter cards on the word builder. Last, child checks their spelling with sound movements.

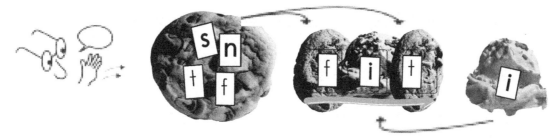

Have child spell the following words changing only one letter at a time for each word: it, sit, fit, fin, in.

 i  t  s f n

Episode 5/Game 10

Blank Page

Word Puzzles - Twin Letter Words

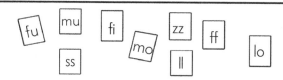

Cut out and mix the cards. Match a cookie and ice cream card to a card with twin letters to make a word.

Fuzz, fuzz, fuzz. My sweater was full of fuzz!

Read the word. Clap it three times and use it in a sentence.

Make two or three words at a time. The words are *fuzz, loss, mutt, off, fill, jazz, miss, moss.*

fu →	zz →	lo →	ss →
mu →	tt →	o →	ff →
fi →	ll →	mo →	ss →
mi →	ss →	ja →	zz →

Episode 5/Game 11

Blank Page

Rhyming Words Trail

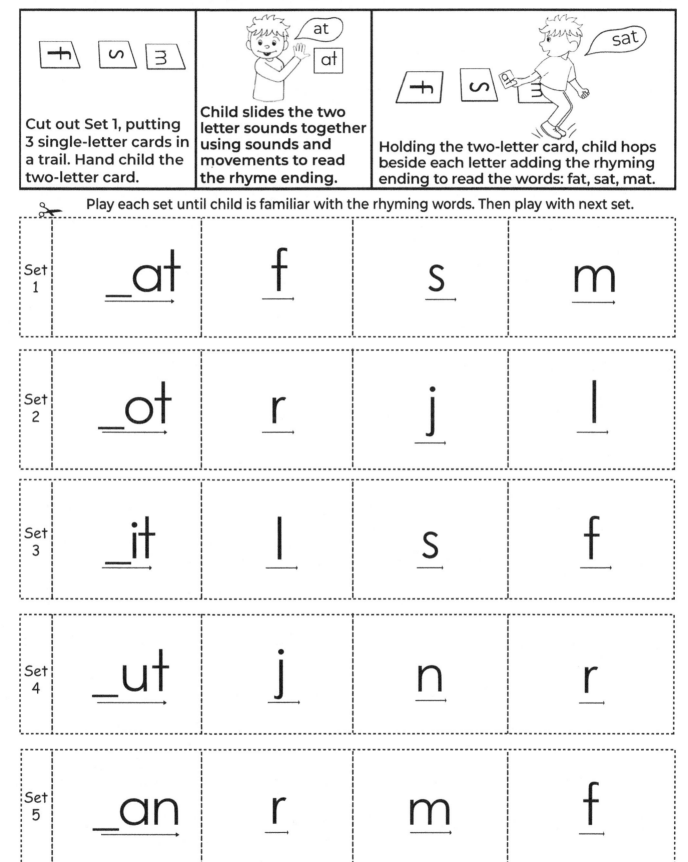

Cut out Set 1, putting 3 single-letter cards in a trail. Hand child the two-letter card.

Child slides the two letter sounds together using sounds and movements to read the rhyme ending.

Holding the two-letter card, child hops beside each letter adding the rhyming ending to read the words: fat, sat, mat.

Play each set until child is familiar with the rhyming words. Then play with next set.

Set 1	_at	f	s	m
Set 2	_ot	r	j	l
Set 3	_it	l	s	f
Set 4	_ut	j	n	r
Set 5	_an	r	m	f

Episode 5/Game 12

Blank Page

Phrase/Picture Match

 **Open Reading**

Read the phrases smoothly. Use the sounds, sound movements, and the "clown sound" movement (one hand on your head), sliding the words together without a break. Remember: the triangle on the word *a* is telling us it is a word with a "clown sound."

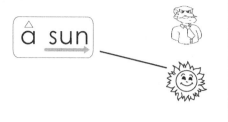

Draw a line from the phrase to the correct picture.

Episode 5/Game 13

Blank Page

Treasure Hunt

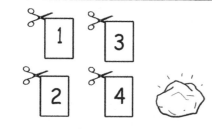

Cut out clue cards. To make a treasure, wrap a snack, coin or small toy in aluminum foil.

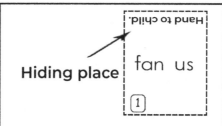

Hiding place

Hiding places are upside down on clue cards. Before the hunt, without the child, hide clues and treasure.

Hand a reading arrow and clue 1 to the child. Give hints during hunt if needed. Have fun!

Hand this clue to child.

fan us

1

Hide this clue by a fan - electric or hand held.

sit on it

2

Hide this clue on a chair.

run on a mat

3

Hide this clue under a mat.
Hide treasure in a cup.

fill it

4

Blank Page

Fletcher Paints Sam

Open Reading

Episode 5

Episode 5: Fletcher Paints Sam

Vocabulary List

Before reading this book, review the list below. Make phrase and word cards on slips of paper so child can hop along a Word and Phrase Trail. Play the Word and Phrase Trail the same as a Sound Trail.

Book Vocabulary Words and Phrases

a mutt

Sam

a mat

a mitt

jam

a fan

fan on

fan off

sit

fun

a mat

3

Make the book

1. To keep the pages in story order, cut the pages from the game book as a group.

2. Then cut the pile of pages along the two cut lines.

3. Remove this page and the vocabulary page from the top of the piles.

4. Begin the book with the cover pile. Then put the next 3 piles below each other following the page numbers.

5. Staple the book along the left side.

Read the book

Have child place a reading arrow below each phrase and slide their finger along the reading arrow as they read.

This book uses phrases. As the child reads, they should not stop between words in a phrase. Child uses the words, phrases and pictures to make up a story.

Blank Page

Episode 5

Fletcher Paints Sam

A Fletcher's Place
Little Book

Colored by:

_____

Story by Irene Hamaker
Illustrated by Matt Beraz
Layout by Cyndy Lemyre

Sam
sit

7

a mitt

4

fun

10

Blank Page

a mutt

1

fan on

8

jam

5

Blank Page

Sam

2

fan on

9

a fan

6

Blank Page

Episode 6: The Treasure Hunt

Overview

Children learn the capital letter shapes for the 14 letters they learned in Episodes 1-5. They learn that capital letters start sentences and periods end them. They read sentences in treasure hunts and in the Little Book.

Episode 6: Fletcher takes everyone on a treasure hunt.

Open video

Reading Skills

- Review 14 letter sounds and lowercase shapes.
- Learn capital letters shapes.
- Focus on the three capital letters that look totally different: *R, A,* and *N.*
- Spell words changing just one letter at a time.
- *Finger slide* under the words, then cover the phrase and read it in the "mind's eye."
- Learn to start a sentence with a capital letter and end with a period.
- Order the phrases of a sentence into first, middle, and last.
- Read treasure hunt clues to draw conclusions about where to find the next clue and the treasure.
- Read the Little Book by reading sentences and talk about fitness.

Sound Guide

a	-	<u>a</u>t
b	-	ro<u>b</u>
c	-	ki<u>ck</u>
d	-	<u>o</u>dd
e	-	<u>e</u>xit
f	-	o<u>ff</u>
g	-	fo<u>g</u>
h	-	<u>h</u>ot
i	-	<u>i</u>t
j	-	<u>e</u>dge
k	-	ki<u>ck</u>
ck	-	ki<u>ck</u>
l	-	hi<u>ll</u>
m	-	a<u>m</u>
n	-	o<u>n</u>
o	-	<u>o</u>ff
p	-	<u>u</u>p
qu	-	<u>qu</u>it
r	-	hai<u>r</u>
s	-	<u>us</u>
t	-	i<u>t</u>
u	-	<u>u</u>p
v	-	lo<u>v</u>e
w	-	o<u>w</u>e
x	-	o<u>x</u>
y	-	happ<u>y</u>
z	-	bu<u>zz</u>
th	-	<u>th</u>is

Review words children can now read:

From Episode 3: **am, an; in, if, on.**
From Episode 4: **fan, jam, man; fin, sis; mom; mum, sum, sun, us, fun.**
From Episode 5:

- Words that begin with *r, v:* **ram, ran, van; rim, run.**
- Words that end with *t:* **at, fat, mat, rat, fit, sat, vat; it, sit, lit; jot, rot, lot, not; jut, nut, rut.**
- Words that end with "twin" consonants: **jazz, mass; ill, fill, sill, mill, fizz, miss, mitt; off, loss, moss; fuss, fuzz, mutt.**
- A word that is a "clown sound" (irregular word): **a.** This word says "uh."

Note: You will find reading arrows on page 7, and on page 401. Use them for reading games. Place them below letters, phrases, words and sentences as you read together.

Episode 6: The Treasure Hunt

	Games to Play	Shown in Episode
1	Read My Hands	Ep. 5: Part 2
2	Letter Puzzles	Ep. 6: Part 1
3	Letter Puzzles	Ep. 6: Part 1
4	Slam Dare	Ep. 6: Part 1
5	Capital/Lowercase Match	not shown
6	Sound Trail	Ep. 4: Part 1
7	Find the Hidden Picture	not shown
8	Memory	Ep. 5: Part 1
9	Fill in the First Letter	not shown
10	Word Trail	Ep. 6: Part 2
11	Fill in the Word	not shown
12	Third Letter Surprise	not shown
13	Sentence Puzzle	Ep. 6: Part 2
14	Treasure Hunt	Ep. 6: Part 3
15	Little Book: Fletcher's Fun Run	Ep. 6: Part 3

Why wait to learn capital letters?
To avoid letter confusion and speed up learning to read, Fletcher's Place teaches lowercase letters first without capital letters. Since most letters in written language are lowercase, the program takes the first five episodes to ensure children master lowercase letter shapes and are reading words. Then, in this episode children need capital letters so they can read sentences.

Why learn to look at the end of a word before reading the word?
Fletcher's Place helps children master the skill of looking ahead to the end of simple words because it is so critical later when reading more complex words. Complex words require looking beyond to the "next letter" to know if the sound will change like /t/ or /th/ in the words _tin_ and _thin_.

Why jump on a Word Trail instead of drilling the sounds with flashcards?
Jumping on a word trail makes practice child's play, is less intimidating, uses their long distance vision and adds the excitement of jumping while also doing the sounds and movements.

Why read three-letter words by only seeing the first two letters and holding out the second letter sound before seeing the third letter?
If three-letter words look scary, it is less intimidating to start by seeing only the first two letters before seamlessly adding the third letter.

Why look ahead at a whole phrase before reading the phrase?
Looking at a whole phrase before reading the phrase helps children read like they speak with a natural spoken, easy to understand rhythm.

How can I get the most out of reading time using the Little Books?
Have children read out loud using the reading arrow and slide their finger under the words to "sneak a peek" at whole phrases. Use sound movements to sound out words as needed and encourage them to use a lot of expression.

Read My Hands

Cut out the cards and place on a table face up. Player 1 silently makes only the sound movements for one word.

Player 2 copies the sound movements, adds the sounds for the word, then points to the matching words in uppercase and lowercase letters.

FAN →	JAM →	VAN →
MILL →	SAT →	RUN →

fan →	jam →	van →
mill →	sat →	run →

Episode 6/Game 1

Blank Page

Letter Puzzles

Cut out letter pieces and mix them up.

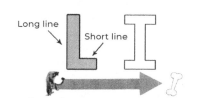

Set the pieces on the letter patterns. Describe each letter piece and then each letter.

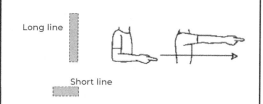

Build the letters without the patterns. Make the sounds and sound movements.

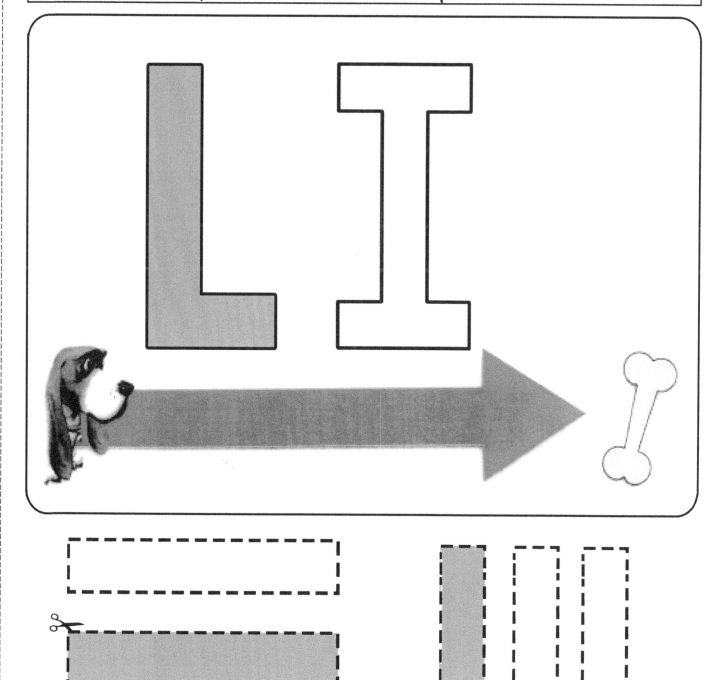

Episode 6/Game 2

Blank Page

Letter Puzzles

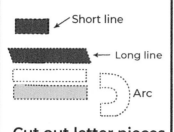

Short line → | ← Long line | Arc

Cut out letter pieces and mix them up.

Long and short lines ARN

Set the pieces on the letter patterns. Describe each letter piece and then each letter.

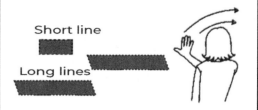

Short line

Long lines

Build the letters without the patterns. Make the sounds and sound movements.

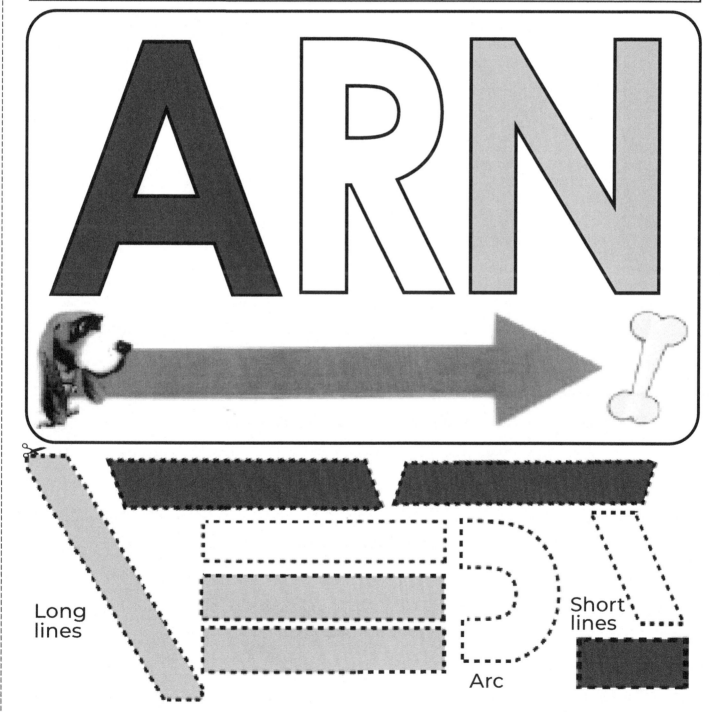

Long lines

Arc

Short lines

Episode 6/Game 3

Blank Page

Slam Dare

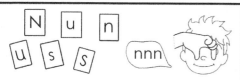

Cut out then spread the letter cards face up. Player 1 makes the sound and movement for a letter sound.

Player 2 slams their hands over the matching capital and lowercase letter cards. Next, Player 1 dares Player 2 to say a word that begins with that sound. Next, Player 2 makes a sound and movement, and Player 1 takes a turn to slam the cards.

A	a	u	u
F	f	L	l
M	m	I	i
N	n	J	j

Episode 6/Game 4

Blank Page

Capital/Lowercase Match

 I	I i 
Say the letter sound and do the sound movement.	Match the capital letter to the lowercase letter.

I
N
F
M
A
L
J
R
T

a
l
f
n
i
j
r
t
m

Episode 6/Game 5

Blank Page

Sound Trail

Cut out the capital and lowercase letter cards. Set them in a trail on the floor.

Jump on each card while making the sound and sound movement.

A	a	u	u
F	f	L	l
M	m	I	i
N	n	J	j

Episode 6/Game 6

Blank Page

Find the Hidden Picture

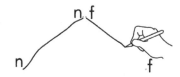

Connect the capital and lowercase letters that make the same sound to find the hidden picture. Do the sounds and sound movements. Color the picture when you are done.

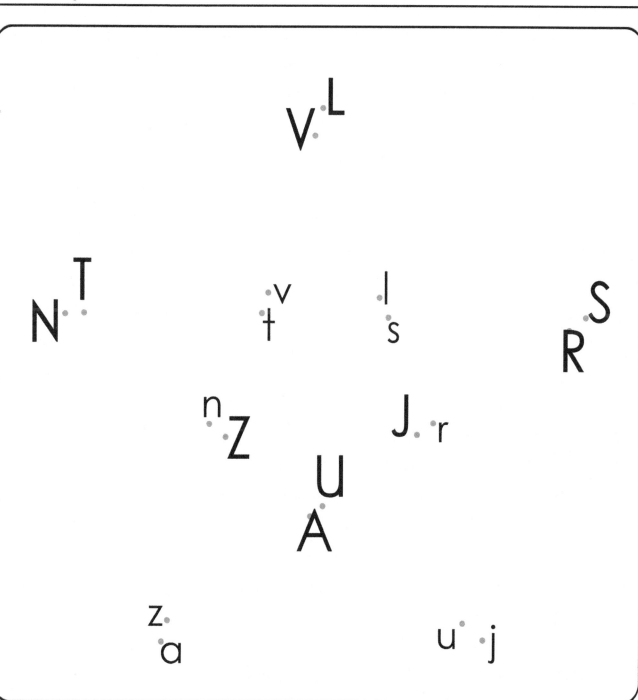

Blank Page

Memory

Cut out the cards. Spread them out face down. Player 1 turns up two cards, does the sounds and movements for each word.

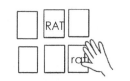

If the words match, Player 1 takes the cards.

If cards do not match, place them face down. Then Player 2 takes a turn.

MISS	RAT	rat	LOT
FUSS	NOT	not	lot
nut	miss	fuss	JOT
FILL	fill	NUT	jot

Episode 6/Game 8

Blank Page

Fill in the First Letter

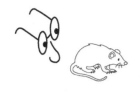 

Look at the picture. Stretch out the word for the picture and do the sound movements.

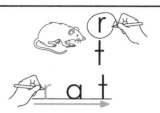

Circle the letter that goes in the blank. Fill in the missing letter. Read the word.

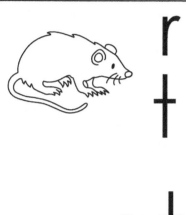

r
t

___ a t

——►

f
v

___ a n

——►

r
z

___ a m

——►

m
n

___ a t

——►

l
r

___ a n

——►

m
n

___ i t t

——►

Episode 6/Game 9

Blank Page

Word Trail

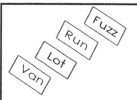

Cut out the cards. Set in a trail on the floor.

Child jumps on each card sliding together the sounds and movements to read the word, clapping the word 3 times. Then they make up a sentence.

Another time, adult bounces a ball to the child, who bounces it on the next word and adult catches it. Child then sounds out the word and makes up a sentence.

Jazz	Lot	Fuss	Van
Ram	Rot	Sit	Mitt
Fit	Rat	Run	Nut
Fizz	Off	Loss	Sat

Episode 6/Game 10

Blank Page

Fill in the Word

Open Reading

 Cut out the words. Place each above a reading arrow. Read them using sounds and movements.	 Place the reading arrow below the sentence. Look at the pictures. Add the correct word to make a sentence.	 Glue the word in the box and read the sentence.

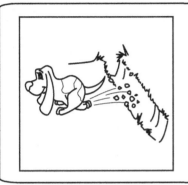   it.

   on it.

   on a mat.

Fill	Run	Sit

177   Episode 6/Game 11

177   Episode 6/Game 11

Blank Page

Third Letter Surprise

Open Reading

 Cut out the 2-letter cards and set them face up in a trail. Set the third letter of each word face down.	Child jumps on each two-letter card, making the movements and sounds holding the second sound untill....	 ... the adult flips over the third sound in each word for the child to seamlessly finish reading the word.

Words made: fa + n, su + n, mo + m, fi + n, ma + n

fa n

su n

mo m

fi n

ma n

Episode 6/Game 12

Blank Page

Sentence Puzzle

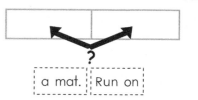

Cut out and set phrases above a reading arrow. Read phrases doing the "clown sound" movement with one hand and the sound movements with the other hand.

Place the two phrases in correct sentence order. Then read the sentence.

a mat.

Run on

Episode 6/Game 13

Blank Page

Treasure Hunt

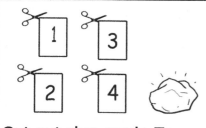

Cut out clue cards. To make a treasure, wrap a snack, coin or small toy in aluminum foil.

Hiding place

Run.
Fill it up.

Hiding places are upside down on clue cards. Before the hunt, without the child, hide clues and treasure.

Hand a reading arrow and clue 1 to the child. Give hints during hunt if needed. Have fun!

Hand this clue to child.

Run.
Fill it up.

1

Hide this clue in a glass or cup.

Run. Sit on a mat.

2

Hide this clue on a mat.

On a ▦ .

3

Hide treasure at a door.
Hide this clue on a shelf.

At a ▯ .

4

Episode 6/Game 14

Blank Page

OpenReading
Episode 6

Fletcher's Fun Run

Episode 6: Fletcher's Fun Run

Vocabulary List
Before reading this book, review the list below. Make word cards on slips of paper so child can hop along a Word Trail. Play the Word Trail the same as a Sound Trail.

Book Vocabulary Words

a	lot
	man
in	miss
it	mom
on	mutt
fill	run
fit	rut
fun	sit

Miss a mitt.

③

Make the book
1. To keep the pages in story order, cut the pages from the game book as a group.

2. Then cut the pile of pages along the 2 cut lines.

3. Remove this page and the vocabulary page from the top of the piles.

4. Begin the book with the cover pile. Then put the next 3 piles below each other following the page numbers.

5. Staple the book along the left side.

Read the book
Have child place a reading arrow below each sentence and slide their finger along the reading arrow as they read.

This is the first book with sentences. As the child reads the story, they should not stop between the words in the sentences.

Blank Page

Episode 6

Fletcher's Fun Run

A Fletcher's Place
Little Book

Colored by:

Story by Irene Hamaker
Illustrated by Matt Beraz
Layout by Cyndy Lemyre

Run on it.

7

Run on a mat.

4

Run in a lot.

10

Blank Page

A fit mutt.

1

Miss a mom.

8

Miss a rut.

5

Run. Run. Run.

11

Blank Page

Run mutt run.

2

Miss a man.

9

Fill a rut.

6

A fit mutt.

12

Blank Page

Episode 7: Fletcher's Campout

Open video

Overview

Children learn the lowercase letter shapes, sounds, and sound movements for four more letters. They distinguish the five vowels from consonants and read "monster words" to practice reading without guessing. They read and follow directions plus read and answer riddles in the <u>Little Book</u>.

Episode 7: Fletcher invites everyone to camp out in his backyard.

Reading Skills

- Use sound movements to connect each letter's common sound to its lowercase shape for *e, g, p,* and *d.*
- Read words ending in "snap sounds" *t, g, p,* and *d* that cannot be held.
- Practice all 5 vowels.
- Read two words that are "clown sounds" (irregular words): *I* and *TV.*
- Sound out nonsense words called "monster words."
- Order *first, middle,* and *last* phrases into sentences.
- Read and follow directions.
- Read treasure hunt clues to draw conclusions about where to find the next clues and the treasure.
- Read the <u>Little Book</u> to learn about hints in riddles and figure out the answers.

Sound Guide

a	-	<u>a</u>t
b	-	ro<u>b</u>
c	-	ki<u>ck</u>
d	-	o<u>dd</u>
e	-	<u>e</u>xit
f	-	o<u>ff</u>
g	-	fo<u>g</u>
h	-	<u>h</u>ot
i	-	<u>i</u>t
j	-	e<u>dge</u>
k	-	ki<u>ck</u>
ck	-	ki<u>ck</u>
l	-	hi<u>ll</u>
m	-	a<u>m</u>
n	-	o<u>n</u>
o	-	<u>o</u>ff
p	-	u<u>p</u>
qu	-	<u>qu</u>it
r	-	hai<u>r</u>
s	-	u<u>s</u>
t	-	i<u>t</u>
u	-	<u>u</u>p
v	-	lo<u>v</u>e
w	-	o<u>w</u>e
x	-	o<u>x</u>
y	-	happ<u>y</u>
z	-	bu<u>zz</u>
th	-	<u>th</u>is

New letter shapes, sounds, and sound movements

e <u>e</u>xit

p u<u>p</u>

d o<u>dd</u>

g fo<u>g</u>

 Note: You will find reading arrows on page 7, and on page 401. Use them for reading games. Place them below letters, phrases, words and sentences as you read together.

Episode 7: Fletcher's Campout

Words children can now read:

Words with *e* in the middle: **fell, sell; jet, let, met, net, set, vet; less, mess.**

Words with *p* at the end: **lap, map, nap, rap, sap, zap; lip, nip, rip, sip, zip; mop; up.**

Words with *g* at the end: **lag, nag, rag, sag, zag; egg, leg, Meg; fig, rig, zig; fog, jog, log; lug, mug, rug.**

Words with *d* at the end: **ad, add, and, fad, lad, mad, sad; fed, led, red; lid; odd, nod, rod; mud.**

Words that are "clown sounds" (irregular words): **I, TV.** In these words, the letters each say their name.

Fletcher's Place teaches words that begin with t, p, d, and g in Episode 8.

Tips

Why wait until now to teach the vowel *e*?
The short-vowel sound for *e* is similar to the short-vowel sound for *i*. To avoid confusion, this program teaches the *e* sound long after children master the *i* sound.

Why can't we "stretch out" the sounds for the letters *t*, *d*, *p*, and *g*?
If children try to "stretch out" these sounds, they will drop their jaw and add an "uh" sound which will distort the word. For example, if children stretch out *pig* by saying "puuuuhiiiiguh," they will not recognize the word.

	Games to Play	Shown in Episode
1	Letter p poster	Ep. 7: Part 1
2	Letter d poster	Ep. 7: Part 1
3	Letter Puzzles	Ep. 7: Part 1
4	Letter Puzzles	Ep. 7: Part 1
5	Sound Buckets- First Sounds	Ep. 2: Part 3
6	5 Flavors of Ice Cream Poster	not shown
7	Sound Buckets-Middle Sounds	Ep. 7: Part 1
8	Read My Hands	Ep. 5: Part 2
9	Match Game: Letters & Sound Movements	Ep. 1: Part 3
10	Memory	Ep. 5: Part 1
11	Word Builder	Ep. 7: Part 2
12	Word/Picture Match	not shown
13	Fill in the Last Letter	not shown
14	Silly Mixed-Up Spelling	Ep. 9: Part 2
15	Monster Words	Ep. 7: Part 2
16	Monster Words	Ep. 7: Part 2
17	Fill in the Word	not shown
18	Crazy Directions	Ep. 7: Part 3
19	Treasure Hunt	Ep. 6: Part 3
20	Little Book: Fletcher's Riddles	Ep. 7: Part 3

Why read nonsense or "monster words?"
Reading words that have no meaning helps children avoid guessing the words and instead focuses on the skill of accurately sounding them out.

Why read "crazy directions?"
Learning to read, understand, remember, and then follow directions is a crucial part of comprehension. Developing this ability with fun "crazy directions" lends a playful tone to this challenging new skill.

Why read riddles?
Riddles give children opportunities to develop their critical thinking and problem-solving skills.

Why "dare" kids to use the words in a sentence? When kids read words, it is important for them to always add meaning to build strong comprehension.

Letter p Poster

Look at the poster for the letter *p*. Remind your child to "pull down the panda balloon."

Do the sound and movement for the letter *p*. Have your child color it and hang it where your child can see it.

Blank Page

Letter d Poster

Look at the poster for the letter d. Remind your child that their fist is a donut and to stick up their thumb so the "donut doesn't roll!"	Do the sound and movement for the letter d. Have your child color it and hang it where your child can see it.

Episode 7/Game 2

Blank Page

Letter Puzzles

	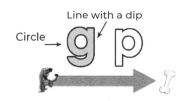	
Cut out letter pieces and mix them up.	Set the pieces on the letter patterns. Describe each letter piece and then each letter.	Build the letters without the patterns. Make the sounds and sound movements.

Episode 7/Game 3

Blank Page

Letter Puzzles

Cut out letter pieces and mix them up.

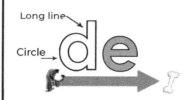

Long line

Circle

Set the pieces on the letter patterns. Describe each letter piece and then each letter.

Long line

Circle

Build the letters without the patterns. Make the sounds and sound movements.

Short line

Long line

Arc

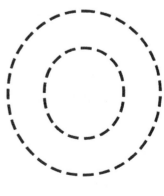

Circle

Episode 7/Game 4

Blank Page

Sound Buckets - First Sounds

Use 2 buckets and a ball for each set. Set 1: Cut out then place the cards *p* and *d* in front of the buckets.	 Adult says a word from Set 1, exagerating the *first* sound.	To figure out the *first* letter, the child repeats the word and makes the sound movement for the *first* sound.	 Child throws the ball in the correct bucket.

Play each set until child is familiar with the *first* sounds. Then play with the next set.

Set 1
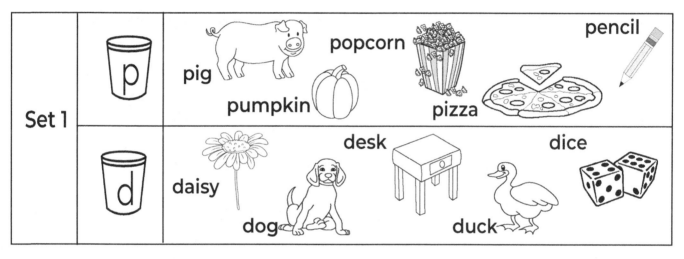

Set 2

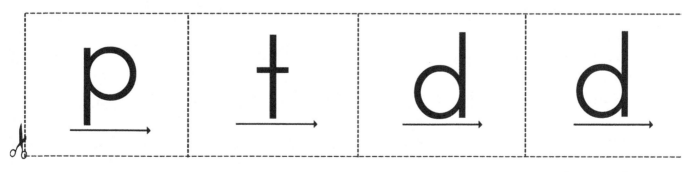

Episode 7/Game 5

Blank Page

5 Flavors of Ice Cream Poster

Look at the poster for the 5 vowels. Use the poster as a memory hook for the rap and song "Short Vowels," seen in Video 7, Part 1.	Do the sounds and movements for the 5 vowel letters: a, e, i, o, u. Have your child color the poster and hang it where your child can see it.

Short Vowel Rap
aaa, eee, iii, ooo, uuu
That's the jive,
The vowels, the vowels
Give me five!

Episode 7/Game 6

Blank Page

Sound Buckets - Middle Sounds

Open Reading

Use 2 buckets and a ball for each set. Set 1: Cut out then place the cards *u* and *a* in front of the buckets.	 Adult says a word from Set 1, making the *middle* sound long and loud.	 To figure out the *middle* letter, the child repeats the word and makes the sound movements for the first two sounds.	 Child throws the ball in the correct bucket.

Play each set until child is familiar with the *middle* sounds. Then play with the next set.

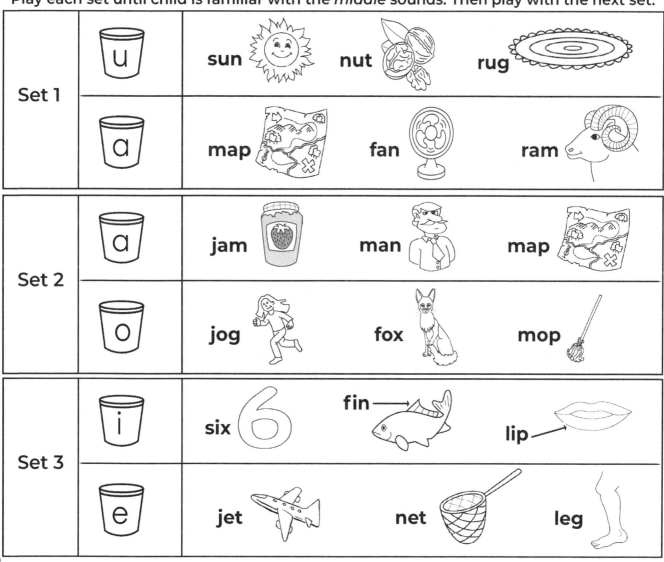

Episode 7/Game 7

Blank Page

Read My Hands

(p, j, u, d, l, e, r, g) **Player 1** silently makes the sound movement for one letter.

Player 2 copies the movement, adds the sound and points to the fish with the correct letter. Then **Player 1** makes another movement.

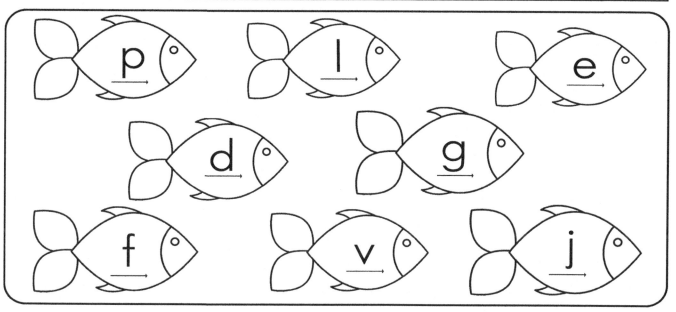

Cut out the cards and place upside down in a pile. **Player 1** picks up a card, silently makes the sound movements for a word without showing it to **Player 2**.

Player 2 does the sound movements with **Player 1** and adds the sounds. When **Player 2** says the correct word, **Player 1** gives the card to **Player 2**.

pig	got	lap
dug	fed	pet

Episode 7/Game 8

Blank Page

Match Game: Letters & Sound Movements

 **Do the sound and sound movement for each letter.**	 **Cut out the sound movement pictures. Do each sound movement.**	 **Glue the sound movements under the correct letter shapes.**

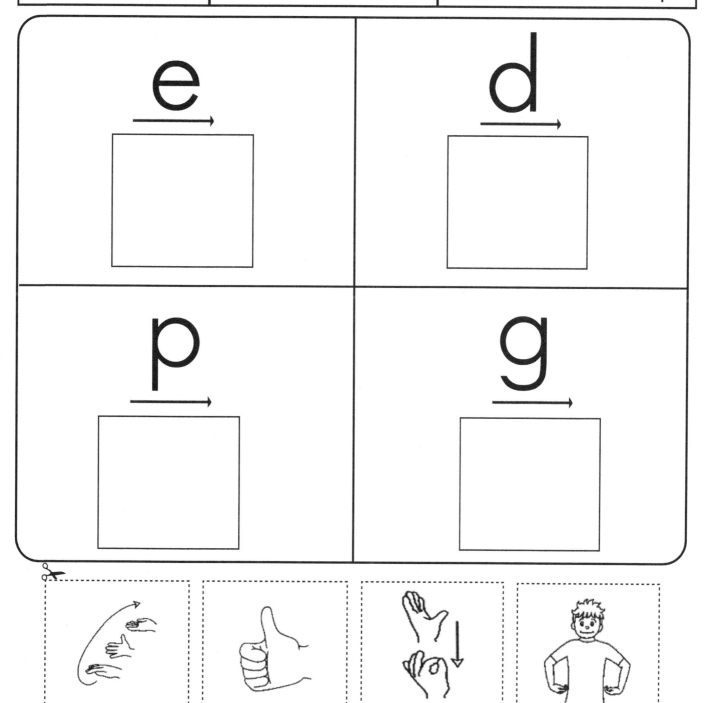

Blank Page

Memory

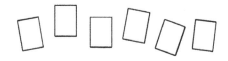
Cut out the cards. Spread them out face down. Player 1 turns up two cards, does the sounds and movements for the letters.

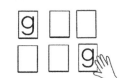
If they match, Player 1 takes the cards.

If cards do not match, place them face down. Then Player 2 takes a turn.

d	e	d	a
g	p	g	r
e	p	t	j
t	j	r	a

Episode 7/Game 10

Blank Page

Word Builder

Cut out the letter cards. Child places the ice-cream vowels on the ice cream and the cookie consonants on the cookie. Do the sounds and movements.

Adult says the word "sag." Child says the word stretching the stretchy sounds, and does the sounds and movements.

Child places the letters on the word builder to spell the word *sag*. Child checks spelling with sounds and movements.

Do the steps for the words sag, rag, rap, sap, sip, rip.

Episode 7/Game 11

Blank Page

Word/Picture Match

Open Reading

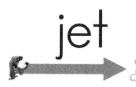 jet

Set a reading arrow below each word. Smoothly slide the sounds and movements together to read each word.

jet

Draw a line from the word to the correct picture.

jet

mop

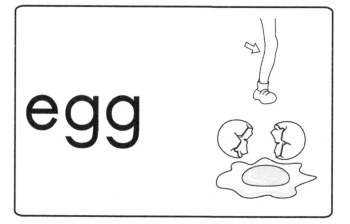

egg

rug

log

lip

Episode 7/ Game 12

Blank Page

Fill in the Last Letter

g		 ru**g**
Cut out the letters below and do the sound movements.	Look at the picture. Stretch out the word for the picture and do the sound movements.	Say each letter sound on the cards. Glue the correct letter to finish each word. Read the word with sounds and movements.

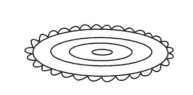

r u ___ →

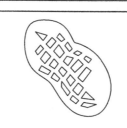

n u ___ →

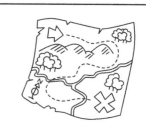

m a ___ →

s i ___ →

n e ___ →

m o ___ →

 g →   t →   t →   p →   p →   p →

Episode 7/Game 13

Blank Page

Silly Mixed-Up Spelling

Cut out the letter cards. Point to the letters on the cookie and ice cream, and have child say the sounds and do the movements.

Adult reads a word from the list below.

Child says the word stretching the stretchy sounds, does the sounds and movements, then spells the word placing the letter cards on the word builder. Last, child checks the word with sound movements.

Have child spell the following words changing only one sound at a time for each word:
leg, led, let, met, mat, mad, lad.

a e l d g t m

Episode 7/Game 14

Blank Page

Monster Words

Set the reading arrow under the monsters' names. Smoothly slide the sounds and movements together to read each name.

Choose eyes and a mouth for each monster. Glue in place.

fom   mep

Blank Page

Monster Words

Set the reading arrow under the monsters' names. Smoothly slide the sounds and movements together to read each name.

Choose eyes and a mouth for each monster. Glue in place.

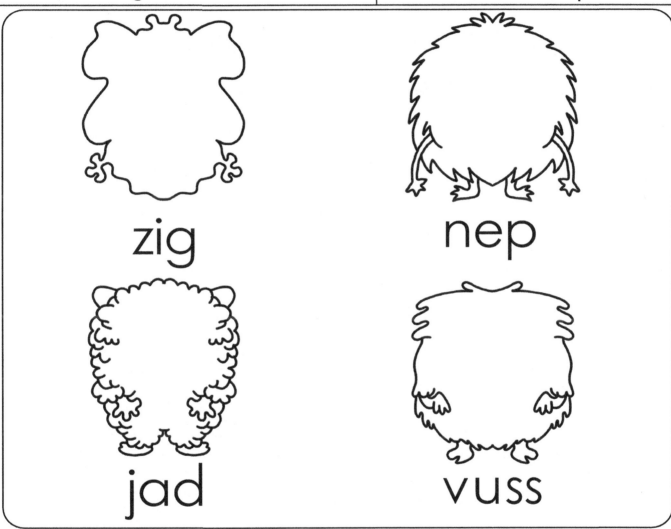

zig

nep

jad

vuss

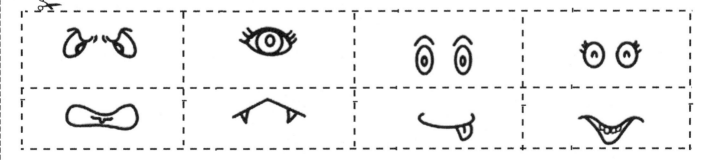

Episode 7/Game 16

Blank Page

Fill in the Word

Cut out the words. Place each above a reading arrow. Read them using sounds and movements.

Place the reading arrow below the sentence. Look at the pictures. Add the correct word to make a sentence.

Glue the word in the box and read the sentence.

Mop up a _____ .

I set a _____ on a TV.

A man _____ on a rug.

| fell | mess | fan |

Blank Page

Crazy Directions

 **Open** Reading

Cut out a set of cards. Get needed props and a reading arrow. Review the words. Set cards face down in a pile. Take turns picking up and reading 1, 2, or 3 Crazy Directions cards.

Set cards aside after reading them. Then act out the directions by memory. Play again with another set.

Props: Set 1 (a cup)   Set 4 (paper, a rug)

Set 1	Nap	Nod	Sip
Set 2	Jog	Run	Sag
Set 3	Sit	Puff	Fan us.
Set 4	Rip it.	Zip it.	Run a lot.
Set 5	Tap a lip.	Nod and nap.	Sit on a rug.

Episode 7/Game 18

Blank Page

Treasure Hunt

 **Open** Reading

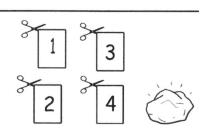

Cut out clue cards. To make a treasure, wrap a snack, coin or small toy in aluminum foil.

Hiding place

Hiding places are upside down on clue cards. Before the hunt, without the child, hide clues and treasure.

Hand a reading arrow and clue 1 to the child. Give hints during hunt if needed. Have fun!

Hand this clue to child.

If mud is

on a leg

sit in a  .

1

Hide this clue in a tub.

I nap in

a 🛏 .

2

Hide this clue next to a bed.

An egg is

🧊

in a 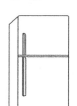 .

3

Hide this clue in a fridge.
Hide treasure in a bowl.

Fill up a .

4

Episode 7/Game 19

Blank Page

Fletcher's Riddles

Episode 7: Fletcher's Riddles

Vocabulary List

Before reading this book, review the list below. Make word cards on slips of paper so child can hop along a Word Trail. Play the Word Trail the same as a Sound Trail.

Book Vocabulary Words

a	am	map
I	in	mutt
TV	it	mug
	on	nap
	up	off
	fill	set
	fit	sip
	jog	sit
		van

I am a mug.

③

Make the book

1. To keep the pages in story order, cut the pages from the game book as a group.

2. Then cut the pile of pages along the 2 cut lines.

3. Remove this page and the vocabulary page from the top of the piles.

4. Begin the book with the cover pile. Then put the next 3 piles below each other following the page numbers.

5. Staple the book along the left side.

Read the book

Have child place a reading arrow below each sentence and slide their finger along the reading arrow as they read.

This book has sentences. As the child reads the story, they should not stop between the words in the sentences.

Blank Page

Episode 7

Fletcher's Riddles

A Fletcher's Place
Little Book

Colored by:

_____

Story by Irene Hamaker
Illustrated by Matt Beraz
Layout by Cyndy Lemyre

Sit in it.

7

I am on.

4

I jog.

10

Blank Page

Fill it up.

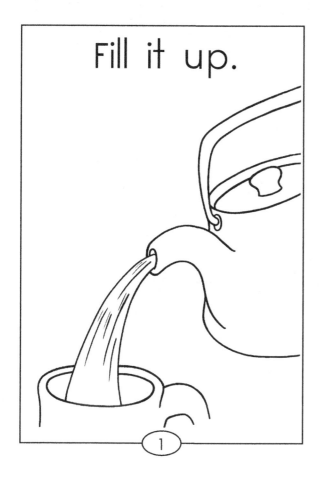

1

Set a map in it.

8

I am off.

5

I nap.

11

Blank Page

Sip it.

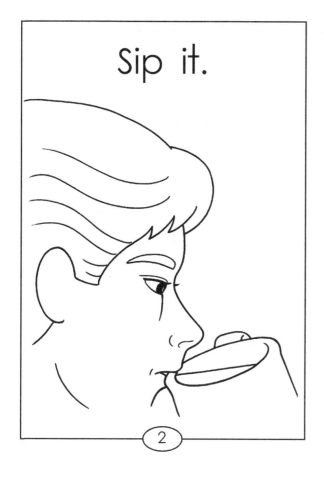

2

I am a van.

9

I am a TV set.

6

I am a fit mutt.

12

Blank Page

Episode 8: Fletcher's Big Mess

Overview

Children learn the lowercase letter shapes, sounds, and sound movements for three more letters. They read words beginning with "snap sounds." They read four-letter words ending in *ck*, and more irregular words.

Episode 8: Fletcher cleans up his big mess.

NOTE: Before beginning Episode 8 where children learn the letter sound and shape for the letter b, be sure they can confidently recognize the shape and sound for the letter d in text around your home. Try looking at street signs and small texts in magazines or on cereal boxes.

Reading Skills

- Use sound movements to connect each letter's common sound to its lowercase shape for *b*, *c*, and *k*.
- Read and spell 4-letter words that end in *ck*.
- Read words that start with the "snap sounds" *t, p, d, g, b, c,* and *k*.
- Read words that have "clown sounds" (irregular words): *be, me, no, so,* and *go*.
- Read phrases and build sentences.
- Read and follow directions.
- Read treasure hunt clues to draw conclusions about where to find the next clues and the treasure.
- Learn the capital letter *G* to read the <u>Little Book</u>. Learn about social justice.

Open video

Sound Guide

a	-	<u>a</u>t
b	-	ro<u>b</u>
c	-	<u>k</u>i<u>ck</u>
d	-	o<u>dd</u>
e	-	<u>e</u>xit
f	-	o<u>ff</u>
g	-	fo<u>g</u>
h	-	<u>h</u>ot
i	-	<u>i</u>t
j	-	e<u>dge</u>
k	-	<u>k</u>i<u>ck</u>
ck	-	ki<u>ck</u>
l	-	hi<u>ll</u>
m	-	a<u>m</u>
n	-	o<u>n</u>
o	-	<u>o</u>ff
p	-	u<u>p</u>
qu	-	<u>qu</u>it
r	-	hai<u>r</u>
s	-	u<u>s</u>
t	-	i<u>t</u>
u	-	<u>u</u>p
v	-	lo<u>v</u>e
w	-	o<u>w</u>e
x	-	o<u>x</u>
y	-	happ<u>y</u>
z	-	bu<u>zz</u>
th	-	<u>th</u>is

New letter shapes, sounds, and sound movements

 **b** rob

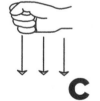 **C** ki<u>ck</u>

 k ki<u>ck</u>

 **ck** ki<u>ck</u>

 *Note: You will find reading arrows on page 7, and on page 401. Use them for reading games. Place them below letters, phrases, words and sentences as you read together.*

Episode 8: Fletcher's Big Mess

Words children can now read:

Words that end with *b*: **jab, fib, rib; job, mob, rob, sob; rub, sub.**

Words that end with *ck*: **lack, rack, sack; neck; lick, sick; lock, rock, sock; luck, muck.**

Words that begin with *t*: **tag, tan, tap; tell, ten; tin, tip; toss, tot; tub, tuck, tug.**

Words that begin with *p*: **pack, pad, pal, pan, pass, pat; peck, peg, pen, pep, pet; pick, pig, pill, pin, pit, pop, pot; puff, pup.**

Words that begin with *d*: **dab, dad; den; did, dig, dim, dip; doc, dog, dot; duck, dug, dull.**

Words that begin with *g*: **gal, gap, gas; get; gob, got; gum.**

Words that begin with *b*: **back, bad, bag, bam, bat; bed, bet, beg, bell; bib, big, bill, bin, bit, boss; bud, bug, bus, but.**

Words that begin with *c*: **cab, can, cap, cat; cob, cop, cot; cub, cup, cut.**

Words that begin with *k*: **kick, kid, kill, kiss, kit.**

Words with "clown sounds" (irregular words): **be, me; go, no, so.**

	Games to Play	Shown in Episode
1	Letter b Poster	Ep. 8: Part 1
2	Sound Buckets - Last Sounds	Ep. 7: Part 1
3	Read My Hands	Ep. 5: Part 2
4	Match Game: Letters & Sound Movements	Ep. 1: part 3
5	Sound Trail	Ep. 4: Part 1
6	Letter Puzzles	Ep. 8: Part 1
7	Letter Puzzles	Ep. 8: Part 1
8	Picture Sort	not shown
9	Memory Words	Ep. 5: Part 1
10	Word/Picture Match	not shown
11	Word Builder	Ep. 8: Part 2
12	Monster Words	Ep. 8: Part 2
13	Fill in the Word	not shown
14	Sentence Puzzle	Ep. 6: Part 2
15	Story Shuffle	Ep. 8: Part 2
16	Story Puzzle	not shown
17	Memory: Words with Clown Sounds	Ep. 5: Part 1
18	Letter Puzzle	Ep. 8: Part 3
19	Crazy Directions	Ep. 7: Part 3
20	Treasure Hunt	Ep. 6: Part 3
21	Little Book: Brad's Big Mess	Ep. 8: Part 3

Tips

Why introduce *ck* now? At the end of one-syllable words, the *k* sound is always spelled with *ck*.

Why wait until now to start using "snap-letter sounds" at the beginning of words?
Starting words with "snap-letter sounds" is harder than adding them to the end of words. For example, to read the word *rob*, the *b* sound is not distorted, but to read the word *bat*, one might add "uh" to the "snap sound," saying, "buhat." This makes the word unrecognizable.

In this episode, children learn to look ahead at the first two letters in the word *bat* and hold them in their mind's eye to smoothly go from the "snap sound" letter "b" to the vowel sound "a" without stopping or adding "uh."

When will the long vowel sounds be taught?
The next level of Fletcher's Place teaches long vowel sounds in longer words. In these 10 episodes children learn long vowel sounds for *e* and *o* as "clown sound" patterns in the words: *be, me, he* and *no, so, go*, and the long vowel sound for *i* in the word that is a "clown sound" *I*.

Letter b Poster

Look at the poster for the letter b. Remind your child that the stick is the person, and he "bumped the ball with his belly."

Do the sound and sound movement for the letter b. Have your child color it and hang it where your child can see it.

Episode 8/Game 1

Blank Page

Sound Buckets - Last Sounds

Open Reading

Use 2 or 3 buckets and a small ball for each set.
Set 1: Cut out then place the cards **g** and **ck** in front of the buckets.

Adult says a word from Set 1, exagerating the *last* sound.

To figure out the *last* letter, the child repeats the word and makes the sound movements for all the sounds.

Child throws the ball in the bucket for the *last* sound.

Play each set until child is familiar with the *last* sounds. Then play with the next set.

Set 1

g — log — bug — pig — dog

ck — duck — neck — sock — lock

Set 2

b — cub — bib — tub — web

d — lid — sad — dad — bed

p — map — pup — up — cap

ck | g | b | d | p

Episode 8/Game 2

Blank Page

Read My Hands

 (p, d, g, e, ck, k, c, b)

Player 1 silently makes the sound movement for one letter.

Player 2 copies the movement, adds the sound and points to the fish with the correct letter. Then Player 1 makes another movement.

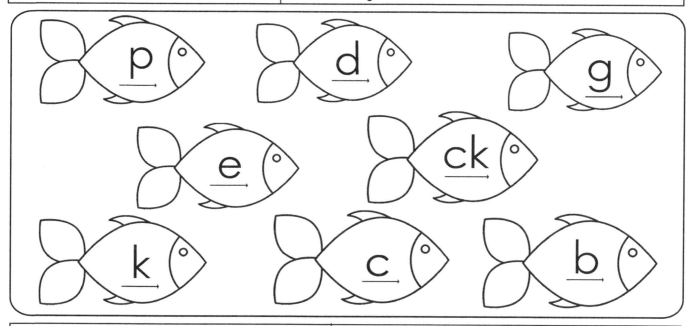

 pet

Cut out the cards and place upside down in a pile. Player 1 picks up a card, silently makes the sound movements for a word without showing it to Player 2.

  pet

Player 2 does the sound movements with Player 1 and adds the sounds. When Player 2 says the correct word, Player 1 gives the card to Player 2.

| pet → | big → | sob → |
| cab → | neck → | kit → |

Episode 8/Game 3

Blank Page

Match Game: Letters & Sound Movements

Do the sound and sound movement for each letter.

Cut out the sound movement pictures. Do each sound movement.

Glue the sound movements under the correct letter shapes.

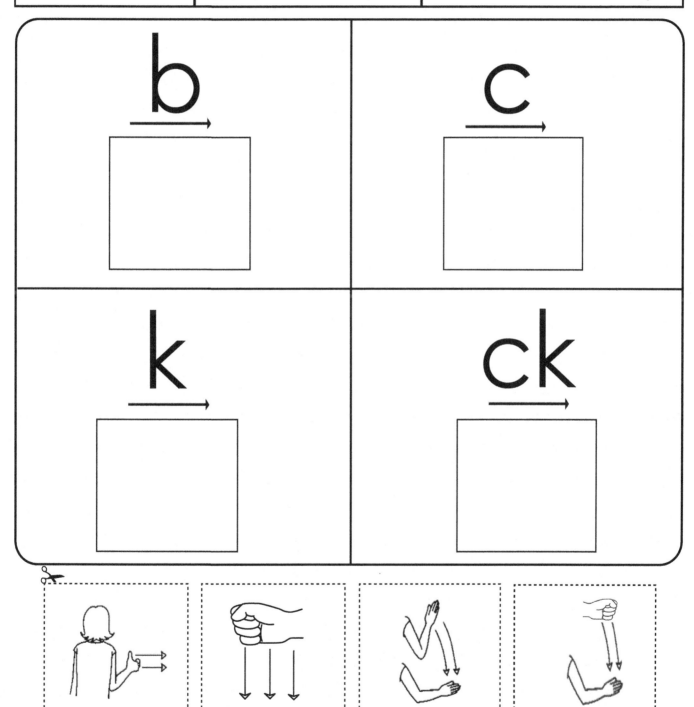

Blank Page

Sound Trail

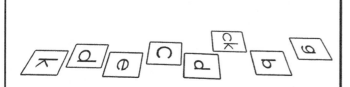

Cut out the cards.
Set them in a trail on the floor.

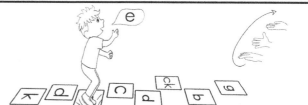

Jump on each card while making the sound and sound movement.

c	c	ck	ck
d	d	k	k
g	b	b	g
e	e	p	p

Episode 8/Game 5

Blank Page

Letter Puzzles

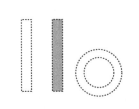

Cut out letter pieces and mix them up.

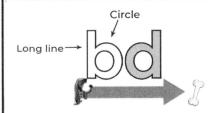

Set the pieces on the letter patterns. Describe each letter piece and then each letter.

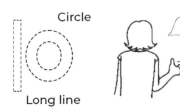

Build the letters without the patterns. Make the sounds and sound movements.

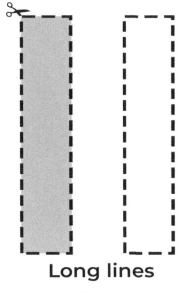

Long lines

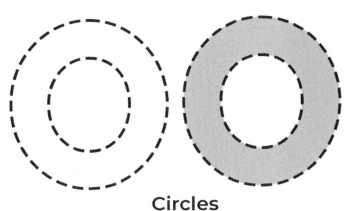

Circles

Episode 8/Game 6

Blank Page

Letter Puzzles

Cut out letter pieces and mix them up.

Set the pieces on the letter patterns. Describe each letter piece and then each letter.

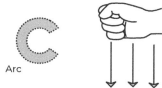

Build the letters without the patterns. Make the sounds and sound movements.

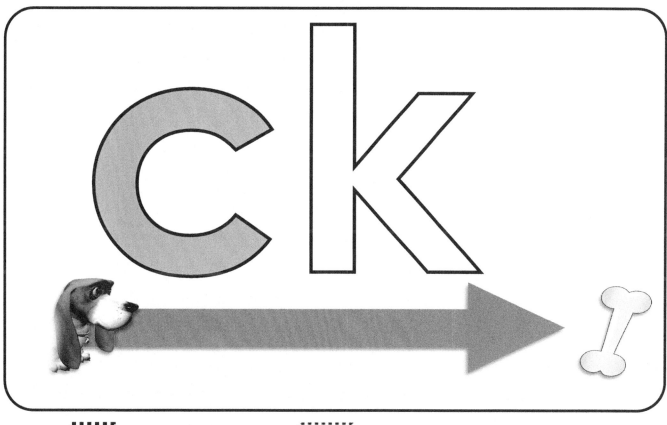

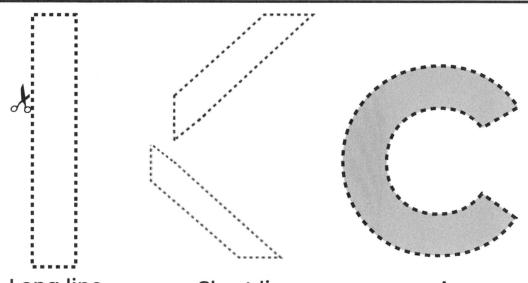

Long line   Short lines   Arc

Episode 8/Game 7

Blank Page

Picture Sort

Open Reading

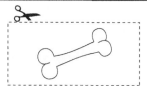

Cut out the picture cards. Say the word. Do the sound and movement for the first sound.

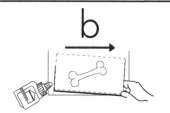

Glue the pictures under the letter that is the first sound in the word.

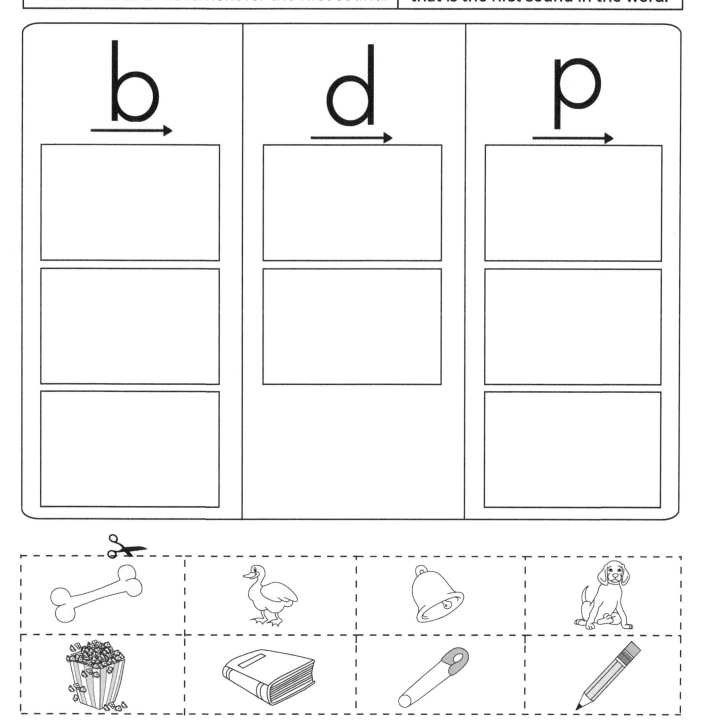

Episode 8/Game 8

Blank Page

Memory Words

Cut out the cards. Spread them out face down. Player 1 turns up two cards, does the sound movements for each word.

If the words match, Player 1 takes the cards.

If cards do not match, place them face down. Then Player 2 takes a turn.

j<u>ob</u> →	d<u>id</u> →	<u>dog</u> →	<u>dog</u> →
t<u>ug</u> →	j<u>ob</u> →	<u>sob</u> →	<u>pill</u> →
<u>sob</u> →	t<u>ug</u> →	<u>did</u> →	<u>pill</u> →
t<u>ell</u> →	<u>pass</u> →	t<u>ell</u> →	<u>pass</u> →

Episode 8/Game 9

Blank Page

Word/Picture Match

 **Open** Reading

Set a reading arrow below each word. Smoothly slide the sounds and movements together to read each word.

Draw a line from the word to the correct picture.

kick

tag

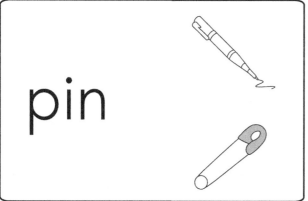

pin

lock

pig

gas

Episode 8/Game 10

Blank Page

Word Builder

Cut out the letter cards. Child places the ice-cream vowels on the ice cream and the cookie consonants on the cookie. Do the sounds and sound movements.

Adult says the word "big." Child says the word stretching the stretchy sounds, and does the sounds and sound movements.

Child places the letters on the word builder to spell the word *big*. Child checks spelling with sounds and movements.

Do the steps for the words big, bag, back, tack, tuck, tub, tug, bug.

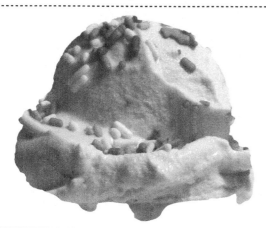 

a	u	i	b	g	t	ck

Episode 8/Game 11

Blank Page

Monster Words

Set the reading arrow under the monsters' names. Smoothly slide the sounds and movements together to read each name.

Choose eyes and a mouth for each monster. Glue in place.

deff

cag

pid

bep

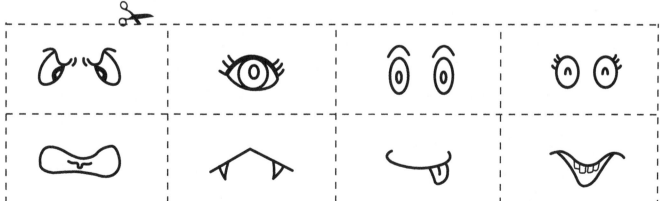

Episode 8/Game 12

Blank Page

Fill in the Word

Cut out the words. Place each above a reading arrow. Read them using sounds and movements.

Place the reading arrow below the sentence. Look at the pictures. Add the correct word to make a sentence.

Glue the word in the box and read the sentence.

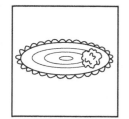 got on a rug.

 Sam fed a _____ a lot.

 I _____ a dog.

 A cat can _____ a dog.

| kiss | duck | Gum | lick |

Episode 8/Game 13

Blank Page

Sentence Puzzle

 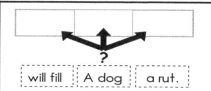

Cut out and set phrases above a reading arrow. Read phrases doing the "clown sound" movement with one hand and the sound movements with the other hand.

Place the three phrases in correct sentence order. Then read the sentence.

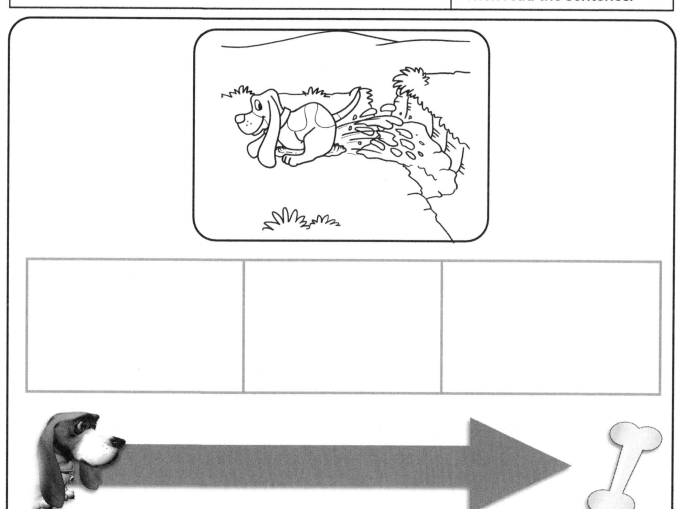

will fill │ A dog │ a rut.

Blank Page

Story Shuffle

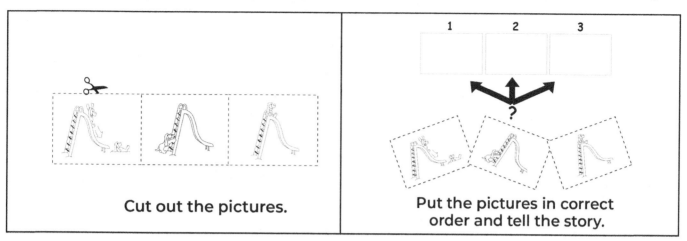

Cut out the pictures.

Put the pictures in correct order and tell the story.

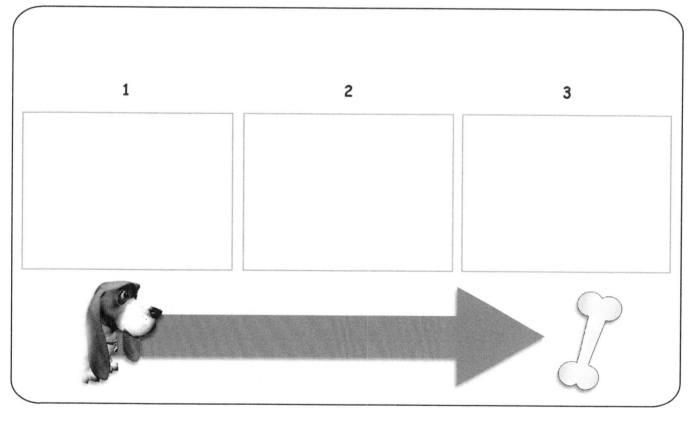

1   2   3

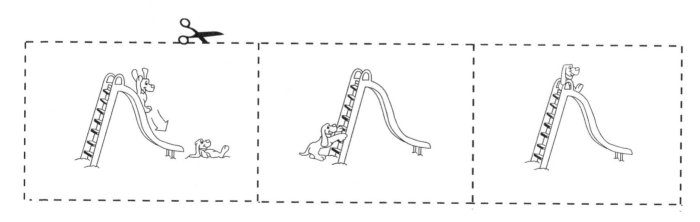

Episode 8/Game 15

Blank Page

Story Puzzle

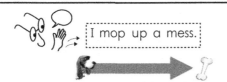

Cut out each sentence. Set each above the reading arrow. Read sentences sliding together the sounds and movements.

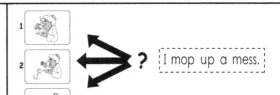

Glue the sentences next to the correct picture to read the story.

1

2

3

I mop up a mess.

I sip it.

It fell.

Episode 8/Game 16

Blank Page

Memory - Words with "Clown Sounds"

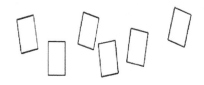

Cut out the cards. Spread them out face down. Player 1 turns up two cards, does the sound movements, and the "clown sound" movement (one hand on their head) for each word.

If the words match, Player 1 takes the cards.

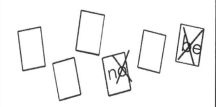

If the words do not match, place them face down. Then Player 2 takes a turn.

no	no	so	so
go	go	me	me
be	be	I	I

Blank Page

Letter Puzzle

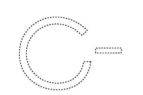		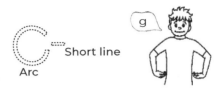
Cut out letter pieces and mix them up.	Set the pieces on the letter pattern. Describe each letter piece and then the letter.	Build the letter without the patterns. Make the sound and sound movement.

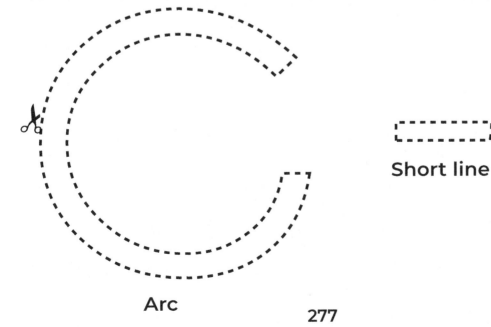

Short line

Arc

Blank Page

Crazy Directions

Cut out a set of cards. Get needed props and a reading arrow. Review the words. Set cards face down in a pile. Take turns picking up and reading 1, 2, or 3 Crazy Directions cards.

Set cards aside after reading them. Then act out the directions by memory. Play again with another set.

Props: Set 2 (cup, rock, TV)   Set 4 (rag, TV, nut, cup)   Set 5 (mat, bag)

Set 1	beg	sob	kiss us	tag us

Set 2	Toss a rock in a cup.	Tap a TV.	Go run.

Set 3	Rub a leg.	Get a bug.	Sit and sob.

Set 4	Rub a rag on a TV.	Set a nut in a cup.	Tap ten taps.

Set 5	Jog on a mat.	Get mad and kick.	Get a bag.

Episode 8/Game 19

Blank Page

Treasure Hunt

 **Open** Reading

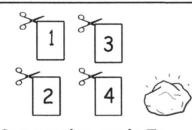

Cut out clue cards. To make a treasure, wrap a snack, coin or small toy in aluminum foil.

Hiding place — Go get gas in it. ①

Hand to child.

Hiding places are upside down on clue cards. Before the hunt, without the child, hide clues and treasure.

Hand a reading arrow and clue 1 to the child. Give hints during hunt if needed. Have fun!

Hand this clue to child.

Go get gas in it.

1

Hide this clue by a car or toy car.

Kiss a mom.

(or)

Kiss a dad.

2

Hide this clue on a mom or dad. (Can be a picture or a person.)

Go get a bag.

It is in a  .

3

Hide this clue in a drawr Hide treasure by a doorbell or other bell.

It is at a bell.

4

Episode 8/Game 20

Blank Page

Brad's
Big Mess

Episode 8

Vocabulary List
Before reading this book, review the list below. Make word cards on slips of paper so child can hop along a Word Trail. Play the Word Trail the same as a Sound Trail.

Book Vocabulary Words

a	bad	jam	sell
be	bat	lot	mess
I	big	mom	toss
TV	can	off	mitt
	cut	red	
am	fun	rip	ick
at	gob	rug	lick
in	get	sad	pack
it	got	set	pick
on	gum	tug	sick
up			

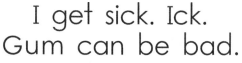

I get sick. Ick.
Gum can be bad.

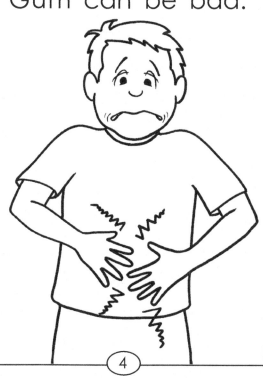

④

Make the book
1. To keep the pages in story order, cut the pages from the game book as a group.

2. Then cut the pile of pages along the 2 cut lines.

3. Remove this page and the vocabulary page from the top of the piles.

4. Begin the book with the cover pile. Then put the next 3 piles below each other following the page numbers.

5. Staple the book along the left side.

Read the book
Have child place a reading arrow below each sentence and slide their finger along the reading arrow as they read.

This book has sentences. As the child reads the story, they should not stop between the words in the sentences.

Blank Page

Episode 8

Brad's Big Mess

A Fletcher's Place
Little Book

Colored by:

_____

Story by Irene Hamaker
Illustrated by Matt Beraz
Layout by Cyndy Lemyre

I cut it off.
Cut.
Cut.
Cut.

9

I set a big
gob on a TV.

5

$ 5.⁰⁰

I get mom
a red rug.

13

Blank Page

Get gum.
Get a lot.

1

I toss it
in a can.

10

6

14

Blank Page

Rip a pack up.

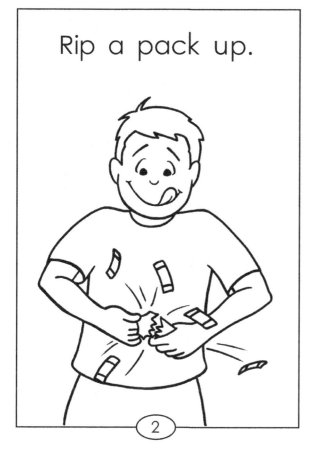

2

Mom is mad.
I am sad.

11

Gum got on
a red rug.

7

Blank Page

I lick it.
I jam it in.

Gum can
be fun.

3

I sell a bat.
I sell a mitt.

12

I tug it.
I pick at it.

8

Blank Page

Episode 9: The Tricky Magic Show

Overview

Children learn the lowercase letter shapes, sounds, and sound movements for the last five letters of the alphabet. They read words beginning with *qu* and ending in *ck*. They learn to ask and answer questions about characters in a story.

Episode 9: Fletcher and Pockets help everyone make magic with reading.

Open video

Reading Skills

- Use sound movements to connect each letter's common sound to its lowercase shape for: *h, y, w, qu,* and *x.*
- Read and spell four- and five-letter words with *qu* and *ck.*
- Read words with "clown sounds" (irregular words): *we, is, his, as,* and *has.*
- Learn story sequence: beginning, middle and end of a story.
- Learn the homonym word *pen* meaning "a pen for pigs," or "a pen for writing." Review the two meanings of the word *fit.*
- Read and follow directions.
- Read treasure hunt clues to draw conclusions about where to find the next clues and the treasure.
- Read the <u>Little Book</u> and learn about recognizing each other's feelings. Focus on characters to ask and answer "who questions."

Sound Guide

a	-	<u>a</u>t
b	-	ro<u>b</u>
c	-	ki<u>ck</u>
d	-	o<u>dd</u>
e	-	<u>e</u>xit
f	-	o<u>ff</u>
g	-	fo<u>g</u>
h	-	<u>h</u>ot
i	-	<u>i</u>t
j	-	e<u>dge</u>
k	-	<u>k</u>ick
ck	-	ki<u>ck</u>
l	-	hi<u>ll</u>
m	-	a<u>m</u>
n	-	o<u>n</u>
o	-	<u>o</u>ff
p	-	u<u>p</u>
qu	-	<u>qu</u>it
r	-	hai<u>r</u>
s	-	u<u>s</u>
t	-	i<u>t</u>
u	-	<u>u</u>p
v	-	lo<u>v</u>e
w	-	o<u>w</u>e
x	-	o<u>x</u>
y	-	happ<u>y</u>
z	-	bu<u>zz</u>
th	-	<u>th</u>is

New letter shapes, sounds, and sound movements

h <u>h</u>ot   **y** happ<u>y</u>   **w** o<u>w</u>e

x o<u>x</u>   **qu** <u>qu</u>it

 *Note: You will find reading arrows on page 7, and on page 401. Use them for reading games. Place them below letters, phrases, words and sentences as you read together.*

Episode 9: The Tricky Magic Show

Words that begin with *h*: had, ham, hat; hem, hen; hid, hill, him, hip, hiss, hit; hog, hop, hot; huff, hug, hum, hut.

Words that begin with *y*: yak, yam, yap; yell, yes, yet; yuck, yum, yip.

Words that begin with *w*: wag, wax; web, wed, well, wet; wig, will, win, wit.

Words that end with *x*: ax, tax; fix, mix, six; ox, box, fox.

Words that begin with *qu*: quack; quick, quill, quit, quiz .

Words with "clown sounds" (irregular words): as, has; he, me, we; is.

	Games to Play	Shown in Episode
1	Read My Hands	Ep. 5: Part 2
2	Letter Puzzles	Ep. 9: Part 1
3	Letter Puzzles	Ep. 9: Part 1
4	Letter Puzzles	Ep. 9: Part 1
5	Letter Puzzles	Ep. 9: Part 1
6	Match Game: Letters & Sound Movements	Ep. 1: Part 3
7	Memory	Ep. 5: Part 1
8	Word Trail	Ep. 6: Part 2
9	Slam	Ep. 2: Part 2
10	Fill in the Word	not shown
11	Word Maze	Ep. 4: Part 1
12	Fill in the Word	not shown
13	Word Builder	Ep. 9: Part 2
14	Silly Mixed-up Spelling	Ep. 9: Part 3
15	Word Toss	Ep. 9: Part 2
16	Word Trail	Ep. 6: Part 2
17	Sentence Puzzle	Ep. 6: Part 2
18	Story Puzzle	Ep. 9: Part 3
19	Crazy Directions	Ep. 7: Part 3
20	Treasure Hunt	Ep. 6: Part 3
21	Little Book: Pug, Ziff, and Fletcher	Ep. 9: Part 3

Tips

How can I help my children pronounce "tricky-letter" sounds accurately?
- Use just your breath to say the "h" sound without adding the sound "uh."
- To pronounce the *y* sound, start and end the sound with your jaw in the same position.
- For *w* do the same, starting and ending the sound with the jaw in the same position.
- The letter sound for *qu*, pronounced "kwww," and letter sound for *x*, pronounced "ksss," are each made of two sounds.

Why is *q* taught as *qu*?
In English, *q* is almost always followed by silent *u* so Fletcher's Place teaches *qu* with the solo (single letter) sounds.

How can I strengthen children's comprehension?
Before reading the Little Book, cover up the illustrations with paper or sticky notes. Have them read the page. Then have them guess what is on the illustration before they see it.

Why ask and answer "who questions?"
Formulating and answering questions is an important part of language development. Learning to identify characters in a story is a primary comprehension skill. To solidify "who questions" have children end their answer by saying, "...that's who." For example: "Who wore the red coat?" "The little girl wore the red coat, that's who."

Read My Hands

(c, x, y, w, qu, h, g) ↓↓↓
Player 1 silently makes the sound movement for one letter.

Player 2 copies the movement, adds the sound and points to the fish with the correct letter. Then Player 1 makes another movement.

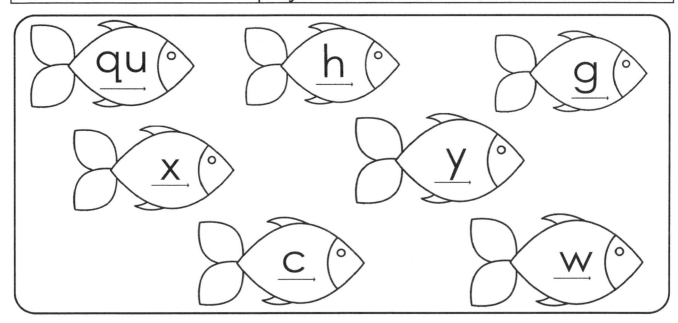

Cut out the cards and place upside down in a pile. Player 1 picks up a card, silently makes the sound movements for a word without showing it to Player 2.

Player 2 does the sound movements with Player 1 and adds the sounds. When Player 2 says the correct word, Player 1 gives the card to Player 2.

quit	hum	fox
wag	yes	quick

Episode 9/Game 1

Blank Page

Letter Puzzles

Cut out letter pieces and mix them up.

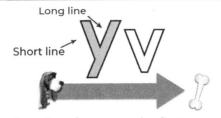

Set the pieces on the letter patterns. Describe each letter piece and then each letter.

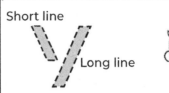

Build the letters without the patterns. Make the sounds and sound movements.

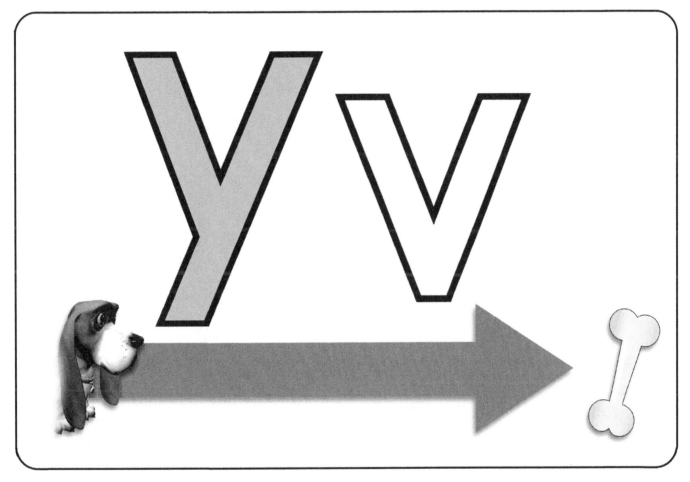

Short lines

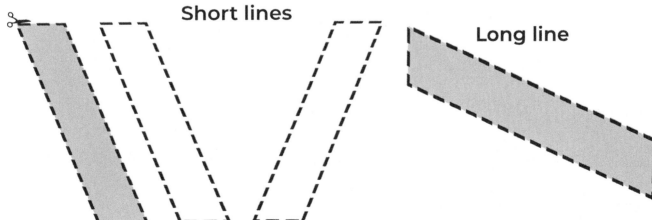

Long line

Episode 9/Game 2

Blank Page

Letter Puzzles

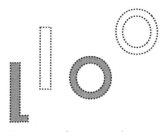

Cut out letter pieces and mix them up.

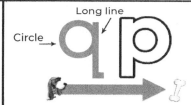

Set the pieces on the letter patterns. Describe each letter piece and then each letter.

Build the letters without the patterns. Make the sounds and sound movements.

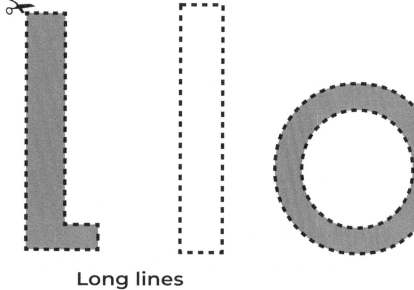

Long lines

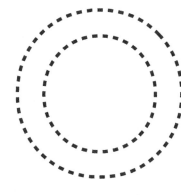

Circles

Episode 9/Game 3

Blank Page

Letter Puzzles

Cut out all letter pieces and mix them up.

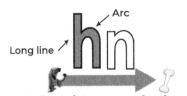
Set the pieces on the letter patterns. Describe each letter piece and then each letter.

Build the letters without the patterns. Make the sounds and sound movements.

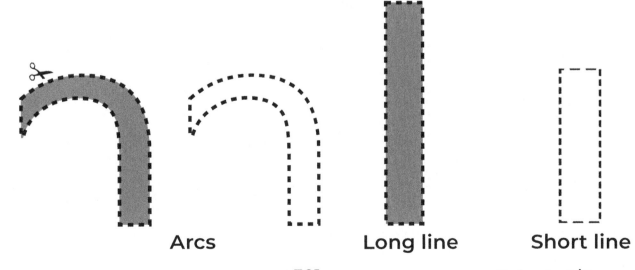

Arcs

Long line

Short line

Episode 9/Game 4

Blank Page

Letter Puzzles

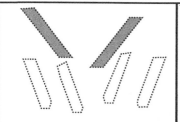

Cut out letter pieces and mix them up.

Set the pieces on the letter patterns. Describe each letter piece and then each letter.

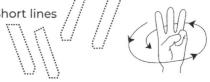

Build the letters without the patterns. Make the sounds and sound movements.

Short lines

Long lines

Episode 9/Game 5

Blank Page

Match Game: Letters & Sound Movements

 Do the sound and sound movement for each letter.	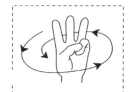 Cut out the sound movement pictures. Do each sound movement.	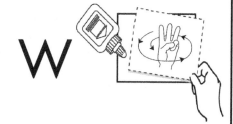 Glue the sound movements under the correct letter shapes.

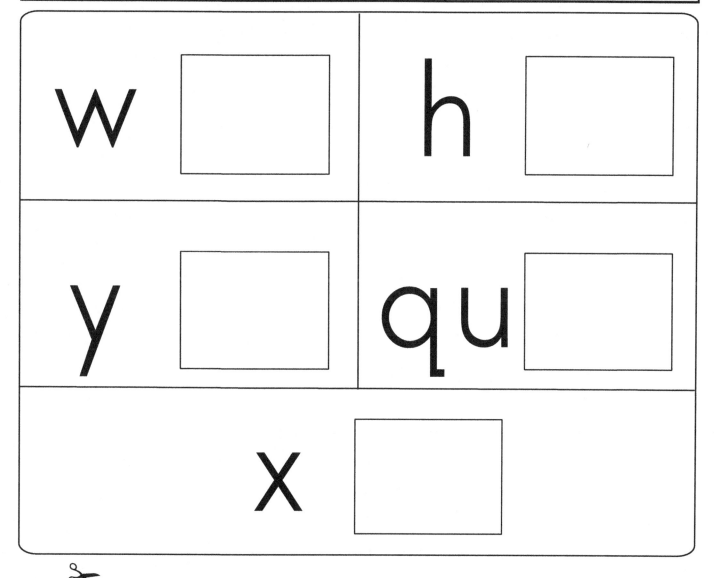

Episode 9/Game 6

Blank Page

Memory

Cut out the cards. Spread them out face down. Player 1 turns up two cards, does the sounds and movements for the letters.

If they match, Player 1 takes the cards.

If cards do not match, place them face down. Then Player 2 takes a turn.

h	y	qu
d	w	x
w	qu	d
y	x	h

Episode 9/Game 7

Blank Page

Word Trail

 Cut out the cards. Set them in a trail on the floor.	 To read each word, child jumps on the cards and says the sounds with the sound movements.	 Dare the child to use each word in a sentence.

wig	fox	yell	hop
quack	wet	mix	yes
quiz	him	win	six
yum	had	quick	hen

Episode 9/Game 8

Blank Page

Slam Words

Cut out then spread out the word cards face up. Player 1 makes the sound movements and sounds for a word.

Player 2 slams their hands over the matching word cards before Player 1 counts to three. Player 2 can then try to slam the cards.

had	yes	hot	wax
yell	wet	had	quit
six	wax	yuck	hen
hot	yes	quit	yuck
wet	six	hen	yell

Episode 9/Game 9

Blank Page

Fill in the Word

Cut out the words. Place each above a reading arrow. Read them using sounds and movements.

Place the reading arrow below the sentence. Look at the pictures. Add the correct word to make a sentence.

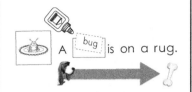

Glue the word in the box and read the sentence.

A [   ] is on a rug.

We will [   ] a cup.

His [   ] is in a box.

A mutt can hop on a [   ].

---

hat   bug   log   fix

Blank Page

Word Maze

 Adult slides a finger along the words from the worm to the apple for Player 2.

 Child reads the words using the "clown sound" movement with one hand (on their head for the "clown sound") and the sound movements with the other hand.

Note to adult: All of these words have "clown sounds."
The "clown sounds" are: o (says its name), e (says its name),
and s at the end of a word (says the zzz).

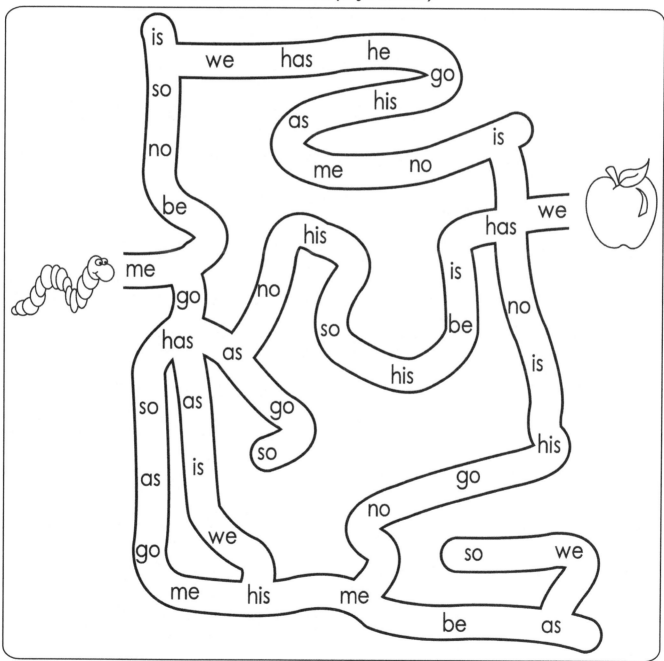

315   Episode 9/Game 11

Blank Page

Fill in the Word

Cut out the words. Place each above a reading arrow. Read them using sounds and movements.

Place the reading arrow below the sentence. Look at the pictures. Add the correct word to make a sentence.

Glue the word in the box and read the sentence.

 We go up a [   ] .

 A bug is on a [   ] .

 He has a [   ] bag.

 I [   ] on an ox.

| big | web | hill | sit |

Episode 9/Game 12

Blank Page

Word Builder

Cut out the letter cards. Child places the ice-cream vowels on the ice cream and the cookie consonants on the cookie. Do the sounds and movements.

Adult says the word "hot." Child says the word stretching the stretchy sounds, and does the sounds and sound movements.

Child places the letters on the word builder to spell the word *hot*. Child checks spelling with sounds and movements.

Do the steps for the words hot, hop, top; yell, yet, pet, wet, and well.

o e h y p t w ll

Episode 9/Game 13

Blank Page

Silly Mixed-Up Spelling

Cut out the letter cards. Point to the letters on the cookie and ice cream, and have child say the sounds and do the movements.

Adult reads a word from the list below.

Child says the word stretching the stretchy sounds, does the sounds and movements, then spells the word placing the letter cards on the word builder. Last, child checks the word with sound movements.

Have child spell the following words changing only one sound at a time for each word:
hit, quit, quick, sick, sit, sat, sack, quack, tack, back, bat, hat.

i a h qu ck t s b

321

Episode 9/Game 14

Blank Page

Word Toss

Adult reads the first word (cat) to the child and tosses them a ball. Child repeats the word and says a sentence. Next, child *action spells* the word with sound movements, and returns the ball.

Adult tosses the ball and says, "Cat. Take off the first sound. What is the word?"
Child does the movments, and removes the sound c and says "at." Child now uses the new word in a sentence, and tosses the ball back. Continue with the remainng pairs of words.

Item needed: ball

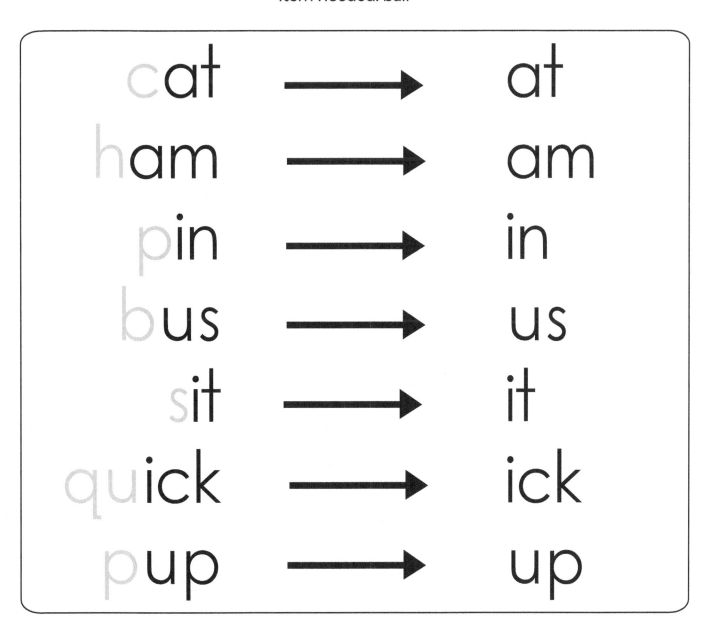

323   Episode 9/Game 15

Blank Page

Word Trail

Cut out the cards. Set them in a trail on the floor.

Child reads the words using the "clown sound" movement with one hand (on their head for the "clown sound") and the sound movements with the other hand as they jump on the cards.

Dare the child to use each word in a sentence.

Note to adult: All of these words have "clown sounds."
The "clown sounds" are: o (says its name), e (says its name),
and s at the end of a word (says the zzz).

as	has	his	he
me	be	is	his
we	go	no	so

Blank Page

Sentence Puzzle

Cut out and set phrases above a reading arrow. Adult finger slides under the phrase and child reads the words using the "clown sound" movement with one hand and the sound movements with the other hand.

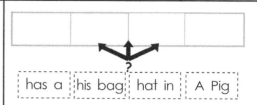

Place the four phrases in correct sentence order. Then read the sentence.

has a | his bag. | hat in | A pig

Episode 9/Game 17

Blank Page

Story Puzzle

Cut out and set each sentence above a reading arrow. Adult slides a finger under the sentence and child reading the words using the "clown sound" movement with one hand and the sound movements with the other hand.

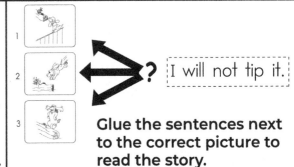

Glue the sentences next to the correct picture to read the story.

1

2

3

A bug is on a log.   A bug is on a dog.

I will not tip it.

Blank Page

Crazy Directions

Cut out a set of cards. Get needed props and a reading arrow. Review the words. Set cards face down in a pile. Take turns picking up and reading 1, 2, or 3 Crazy Directions cards.

Set cards aside after reading them. Then act out the directions by memory.

Props: Set 2 (water) Set 3 (pretend ham) Set 4 (rock, sock, bag, tub)

| Set 1 | hum | hiss | yell | hop |

| Set 2 | yell no | get wet | nod yes | hit a leg |

Set 3

| Tap a neck. | Get up and hiss. |
| Sell me a ham. | Hop and sit. |

Set 4

Set a rock on a sock.

Tell me if mud is wet.

Get in a tub.

Rip a big bag.

Blank Page

Treasure Hunt

 **Open** Reading

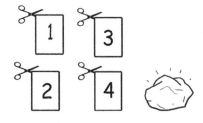

Cut out clue cards. To make a treasure, wrap a snack, coin or small toy in aluminum foil.

Hiding place

Hiding places are upside down on clue cards. Before the hunt, without the child, hide clues and treasure.

Hand a reading arrow and clue 1 to the child. Give hints during hunt if needed. Have fun!

Hand this clue to child.

A nut is in
a cup.

1

Hide clue in a cup, with or without nuts.

It is not lit but
it has wax.

2

Hide clue near a candle.

Jam can be in it.
A hot dog can be in it.
A dip can be in it.

3

Hide clue in a fridge.
Hide treasure in a tub.

It has mud on it.
Get it wet in a tub.

4

Episode 9/Game 20

Blank Page

Open Reading
Episode 9

Pug, Ziff, and Fletcher

Episode 9: Pug, Ziff, and Fletcher

Vocabulary List
Before reading this book, review the list below. Make word cards on slips of paper so child can hop along a Word Trail. Play the Word Trail the same as a Sound Trail.

Book Vocabulary Words

a	in	leg	will
I	it	log	yell
	on	mad	Ziff
he	us	mud	
me	and	not	muck
we	bit	pal	yuck
	bug	pen	
so	can	pig	Fletcher
no	dog	Pug	
	get	rug	
is	got	run	
has	hop	tip	
his	hug	wet	

A rug is
on a log.

On it is Ziff.
He is a bug.

3

Make the book
1. To keep the pages in story order, cut the pages from the game book as a group.

2. Then cut the pile of pages along the 2 cut lines.

3. Remove this page and the vocabulary page from the top of the piles.

4. Begin the book with the cover pile. Then put the next 3 piles below each other following the page numbers.

5. Staple the book along the left side.

Read the book
Have child place a reading arrow below each sentence and slide their finger along the reading arrow as they read.

This book has sentences. As the child reads the story, they should not stop between the words in the sentences.

Blank Page

Episode 9

Pug, Ziff, and Fletcher

A Fletcher's Place
Little Book

Colored by:

_____

Story by Irene Hamaker
Illustrated by Matt Beraz
Layout by Cyndy Lemyre

Pug has a pal.
His pal is Fletcher.

Blank Page

Pug is
a pig.

1

Ziff will
get mad.

He will yell.

Not on me.
It will tip.

8

Run in
so we
can hug.

Not me.
Mud is muck.
Muck is yuck.

5

A bug
is on
his rug.

11

Blank Page

His pen has mud.
A log is in his pen.

2

I will not
tip it.

9

Mud is wet.

Fletcher
will not
get mud
on his leg.

6

No mud
got on us.
Not a bit.

12

Blank Page

Episode 10: The Sky's the Limit

Open Reading

Open video

Overview

Children learn the remaining capital letter shapes and all letter names. They learn the "partner" th. They can now read 300 regularly spelled words plus 20 irregular words in phrases and sentences. They learn to ask and answer questions about locations in a story.

Episode 10: Fletcher's friends talk about what they want to be when grown up.

Reading Skills

- Review all 26 letters sounds, lowercase shapes, and sound movements.
- Learn the remaining capital letter shapes: *B, K, Y, C, W, P, H, E, D, N, Qu,* and *X*. Focus on the five capital letters that look totally different from the lowercase letter shapes: *H, E, D, N,* and *Qu*.
- Learn all 26 letter names.
- Use the "partner" sound movement to connect the most common sound for the "partner" letters *th*.
- Read irregular words: *the, to, do, my* and *by*.
- Read and follow directions.
- Read more advanced treasure hunt clues to draw conclusions about where to find the next clues and the treasure.
- Read the <u>Little Book</u> to learn about actions and consequences. Focus on locations to ask and answer "where questions."

Sound Guide

a	-	<u>a</u>t
b	-	ro<u>b</u>
c	-	<u>k</u>ick
d	-	o<u>dd</u>
e	-	<u>e</u>xit
f	-	o<u>ff</u>
g	-	fo<u>g</u>
h	-	<u>h</u>ot
i	-	<u>i</u>t
j	-	e<u>dge</u>
k	-	ki<u>ck</u>
ck	-	ki<u>ck</u>
l	-	hi<u>ll</u>
m	-	a<u>m</u>
n	-	o<u>n</u>
o	-	<u>o</u>ff
p	-	u<u>p</u>
qu	-	<u>qu</u>it
r	-	hai<u>r</u>
s	-	u<u>s</u>
t	-	i<u>t</u>
u	-	<u>u</u>p
v	-	lo<u>v</u>e
w	-	o<u>w</u>e
x	-	o<u>x</u>
y	-	happ<u>y</u>
z	-	bu<u>zz</u>
th	-	<u>th</u>is

New "partner" sound, and sound movement.

th <u>th</u>is

Make the *th* sound movement by placing your thumb over the top of your fist, like your tongue sticks out over your teeth.

Note: You will find reading arrows on page 7, and on page 401. Use them for reading games. Place them below letters, phrases, words and sentences as you read together.

Episode 10: The Sky's the Limit

Words children can now read:

Three-letter words that begin with a vowel: **act, and, ant, ask; elf, elk, elm, end.**

A word with a "clown sound" (irregular word): **the.** The letter *e* says "uh:"

Words with "clown sounds" (irregular words): **by, my; do, to.**

	Games to Play	Shown in Episode
1	Sound and Name Trail	Ep. 10: Part 1
2	Sound and Name Trail	Ep. 10: Part 1
3	Sound and Name Trail	Ep. 10: Part 1
4	Sound and Name Trail	Ep. 10: Part 1
5	Letter Puzzles	Ep. 10: Part 2
6	Letter Puzzles	Ep. 10: Part 2
7	Letter Puzzles	Ep. 10: Part 2
8	Super Name Slam	Ep. 10: Part 2
9	Super Name Memory	Ep. 5: Part 1
10	Capital/Lowercase Match	not shown
11	Fill in the Word	not shown
12	Word Trail	Ep. 6: Part 2
13	Word Toss	Ep. 10: Part 3
14	Word Trail	Ep. 6: Part 2
15	Crazy Directions	Ep. 7: Part 3
16	Treasure Hunt	Ep. 10: Part 3
17	Bonus Treasure Hunt	Ep. 10: Part 3
18	<u>Little Book: Fletcher and the Vet</u>	Ep. 10: Part 3

Tips

How do we make it easy to learn letter names?
We teach letter names in four groups based on the pattern for how they include or don't include the letter's common sound:

1. Vowel names which are not related to the common letter sound (the short vowel sound): *a, e, i, o, u.*
2. Consonant names which start with the common letter sound like the letter *b*, pronounced "<u>bee</u>:" *b, d, j, k, p, t, v, z.*
3. Consonant names which end with the common letter sound like the letter *m*, pronounced "<u>em</u>:" *f, l, m, n, r, s, x.*
4. Consonant names which are not related to the common letter sound like *h* pronounced "aich:" *c, g, h, q, w, y.*

Should I refer to a "larger letter shape" as a capital letter or an uppercase letter?
Have children get used to using them both.

What is the "sound" awareness skill children learn playing Word Toss?
Children become aware of individual sounds within a word, and when the sound is changed, the meaning of the word changes. When they say a word like "hat," then change the last sound *t* to *m*, they are now saying "ham."

Why ask and answer "where questions?"
Formulating and answering questions about setting is one of the primary comprehension skills. To solidify "where questions," have children end their answer by saying, "...that's where." For example: "Where did the princess live?" "The princess lived in the castle, that's where."

Sound and Name Trail

Cut out the cards for the letter names that start with their sound. Set them in a trail on the floor.

Child jumps on each card, does the sound movement, says the sound, and then says the letter name.

p	t	v
j	k	z
b	d	

Episode 10/Game 1

Blank Page

Sound and Name Trail

Cut out the cards for the letter names that end with their sound. Set them in a trail on the floor.

Child jumps on each card, does the sound movement, says the sound, and then says the letter name.

n	f	m
x	s	r
l		

Episode 10/Game 2

Blank Page

Sound and Name Trail

Cut out the cards for the letters with names that "make no sense at all!" Set them in a trail on the floor.

c (ck) is the sound.
See is the name.

Child jumps on each card, does the sound movement, says the sound, and then says the letter name.

c

w

h

y

g

qu

Episode 10/Game 3

Blank Page

Sound and Name Trail

Cut out the cards for the vowel letters. Set them in a trail on the floor.

Child jumps on eacn card, does the sound movement, says the sound, and then says the letter name.

a

e

i

o

u

Blank Page

Letter Puzzles

Open Reading

Cut out letter pieces and mix them up.

Set the pieces on the letter patterns. Describe each letter piece and then each letter.

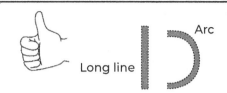
Build the letters without the patterns. Make the sounds and sound movements.

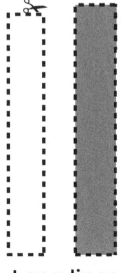
Long lines

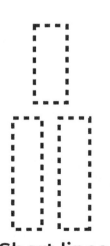
Short lines

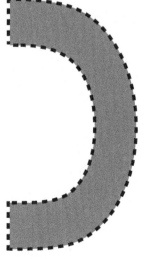
Arc

Episode 10/Game 5

Blank Page

Letter Puzzles

Cut out letter pieces and mix them up.

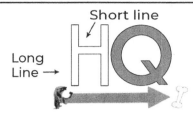

Set the pieces on the letter patterns. Describe each letter piece and then each letter.

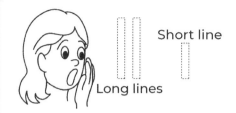

Build the letters without the patterns. Make the sounds and sound movements.

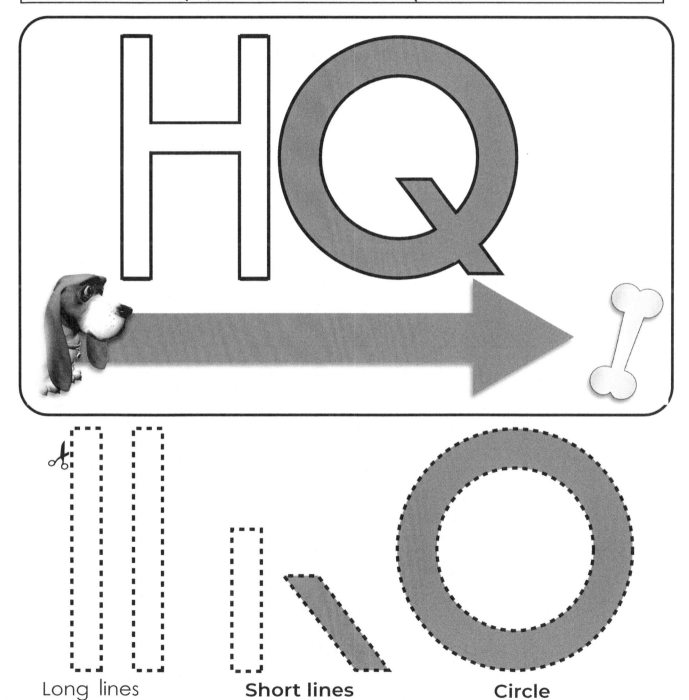

Long lines

Short lines

Circle

Episode 10/Game 6

Blank Page

Letter Puzzles

Cut out letter pieces and mix them up.

Long line **M** Long slanted line **W**

Set the pieces on the letter patterns. Describe each letter piece and then each letter.

Build the letters without the patterns. Make the sounds and sound movements.

Long slanted line

Long line

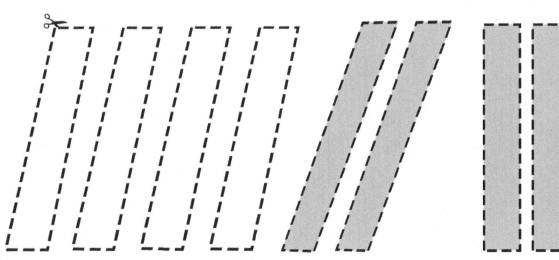

Long slanted lines   **Long lines**

357

Episode 10/Game 7

Blank Page

Super Name Slam

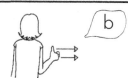 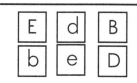 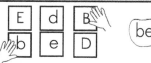 

Cut out then spread out the letter cards face up. Player 1 does the sound and sound movement for a letter.

Player 2 slams their hands over the matching capital and lowercase letter cards and says the letter's name. Next, Player 2 makes a sound and movement, and Player 1 takes a turn.

E→	D→	B→	Qu→
e→	d→	b→	qu→
H→	G→	W→	M→
h→	g→	w→	m→

Episode 10/Game 8

Blank Page

Super Name Memory

Cut out the cards and place them face down. Player 1 turns up two cards, does the movement, says the sound and name for the letters.

If the upper and lowercase letters match, Player 1 takes the cards.

If cards do not match, place them face down. Then Player 2 takes a turn.

A	F	I	L
a	f	i	l
N	R	T	u
n	r	t	u

Episode 10/Game 9

Blank Page

Capital/Lowercase Match

 E

Say the letter sound and do the sound movement.

E——e

Match the capital letter to the lower-case letter.

E

K

H

Y

B

D

G

Qu

k

y

g

qu

e

h

b

d

Episode 10/Game 10

Blank Page

Fill in the Word

Cut out and place each word above a reading arrow. Read them using sound movements and the clown sound movement.

Place the reading arrow below the sentence. Look at the pictures.

Glue the correct word to make a sentence and read it.

I fell in the _____ .

My _____ is cut.

We can _____ mud off.

The _____ can fix the cut.

| mud | vet | leg | rub |

Episode 10/Game 11

Blank Page

Word Trail

 Cut out the word cards. Set them in a trail on the floor. Have a reading arrow ready if needed.	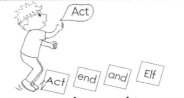 Jump on each word to read it, saying sounds and doing movements without a break.	 Dare the trail hopper to use each word in a sentence.

ACT →	END →	AND →
ANT →	ASK →	ELF →
ELK →	ELM →	AX →
OX →	UP →	US →

Episode 10/Game 12

Blank Page

Word Toss

Adult reads the first word (bit) out loud and tosses a ball to the child. Child repeats the word, uses it in a sentence, then tosses the ball back.

Adult repeats the word and asks the child to change the first or last sound. Adult tosses the ball to the child. Child says new word, uses it in a sentence, and tosses the ball back.

Item needed: ball

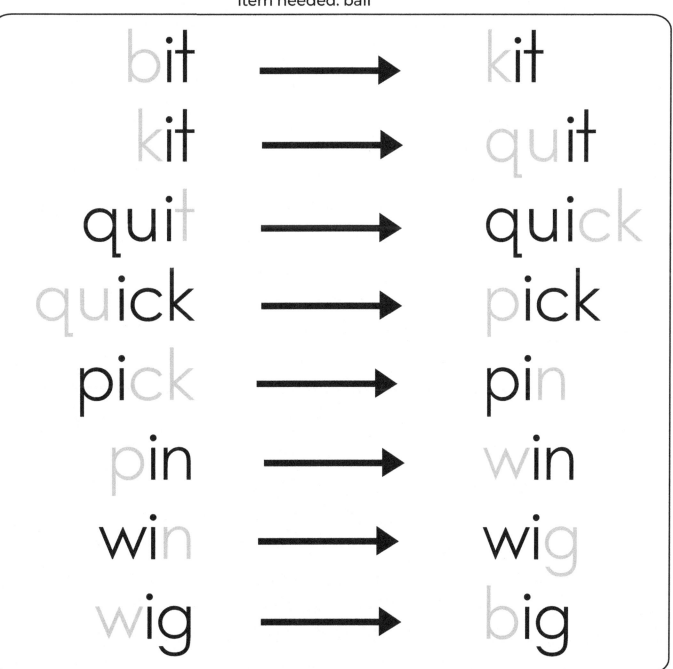

Episode 10/Game 13

Blank Page

Word Trail

Cut out the cards for the words with _clown sounds_. Set them in a trail on the floor.

To read each word, child jumps on the card, does the sound movements and the _clown sound_ movement (patting their head) as they read each word.

Dare the child to use each word in a sentence.

the	THE	do	to
BY	MY	be	me
WE	he	NO	GO

Blank Page

Crazy Directions

Open Reading

| Huff and puff. |
| Do six hops. |
| Do a zig zag run. |

Cut out a set of cards. Get needed props and a reading arrow. Review the words. Set cards face down in a pile. Take turns picking up and reading 1, 2, or 3 Crazy Directions cards.

Hhh! Pfff! 1, 2, 3, 4, 5, 6!

Set cards aside after reading them. Then act out the directions by memory. Play again with another set.

Props: Set 2 (cup, sack, bell) Set 3 (bed, rag, pen) Set 4 () Set 5 (water, hat)

Set 1

| Do six hops. | Do a zig zag run. |
| Huff and puff. | Do ten kicks. |

Set 2

| Add ten and six. | Hit a bell and sob. |
| Toss a sack to me. | Pass a cup to me. |

Set 3

Tell me if it is hot.	Set a pen in my lap.
Jog up to a bed and hop on it.	
Get a rag and dab my neck.	

Set 4

| It is hot so fan us. | Nod if a cat will hiss. |
| Tell me if wax can get hot. | |

Set 5

Act hot and get wet.	Fix the rim on my hat.
Ask me if a hog and pig can kiss.	
Tell me if an ant can yell.	

Episode 10/Game 15

Blank Page

Treasure Hunt

Open Reading

 1 3 2 4	**Hiding place** → Kick it. Toss it up. It is a b___.	

Cut out clue cards. To make a treasure, wrap a snack, coin or small toy in aluminum foil.

Hiding places are upside down on clue cards. Before the hunt, without the child, hide clues and treasure.

Hand a reading arrow and clue 1 to the child. Give hints during hunt if needed. Have fun!

Hand this clue to child.

Kick it.
Toss it up.
It is a b__ __ __.

1

Hide this clue under a ball.

Get a pen.
Jot on it.
I can toss it
in the can if
I mess up.

2

Hide this clue under a piece of paper.

Tick tock.
Tick Tock.
I am a c____.

3

Hide this clue by a clock.
Hide treasure by a pillow.

I can be
on a bed.
Hug me.
Sit on me.
I am a p____.

4

Blank Page

Bonus Treasure Hunt

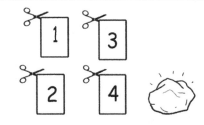

Cut out clue cards. To make a treasure, wrap a snack, coin or small toy in aluminum foil.

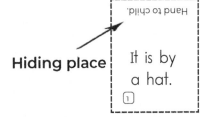

Hiding place

It is by a hat.

Hiding places are upside down on clue cards. Before the hunt, without the child, hide clues and treasure.

Hand a reading arrow and clue 1 to the child. Give hints during hunt if needed. Have fun!

Hand this clue to child.

It is by a hat.

1

Hide this clue by a hat.

Pick it up. Lick it. Yum.

2

Hide this clue with food that can be licked.

It is in a box but do not get it wet.

3

Hide this clue in a box set in a sink
Hide treasure four hops away from the mat.

Sit on a mat. Get up and hop ten hops. Hop back six.

4

Blank Page

Open Reading

Fletcher and the Vet

Episode 10

4

Vocabulary List
Before reading this book, review the list below. Make word cards on slips of paper so child can hop along a Word Trail. Play the Word Trail the same as a Sound Trail.

Book Vocabulary Words

a	am	job	van
I	in	log	vet
me	is	leg	wag
we	it	let	
be	on	mud	off
no	us	not	Ziff
go	and	pen	mess
so	bad	Pug	fell
by	bug	red	will
my	can	rub	well
to	cut	sad	back
has	fix	sit	yuck
his	get	sob	quit
the	hit	tip	quick

Make the book
1. To keep the pages in story order, cut the pages from the game book as a group.

2. Then cut the pile of pages along the 2 cut lines.

3. Remove this page and the vocabulary page from the top of the piles.

4. Begin the book with the cover pile. Then put the next 3 piles below each other following the page numbers.

5. Staple the book along the left side.

Read the book
Have child place a reading arrow below each sentence and slide their finger along the reading arrow as they read.

This book has sentences. As the child reads the story, they should not stop between the words in the sentences.

Blank Page

Episode 10

Fletcher and the Vet

A Fletcher's Place
Little Book

Colored by:

_____

Story by Irene Hamaker
Illustrated by Matt Beraz
Layout by Cyndy Lemyre

Blank Page

Blank Page

2

11

7

Blank Page

Blank Page

Lyrics for All Songs

Episode 1

Song 1. Introduction
We're On Our Way to Fletcher's Place

Chorus
We're on our way to Fletcher's Place!

Song 2.
Look Up, Top-Down, Left to Right: Word Stretch

Chorus
Look up, top-down, left to right,
Word stretch,
Bring it tight,
Out of sight.
(REPEAT)

Verse
Stretch the magic collar,
Streeeetch out words.
Hold out the sound
So every sound is heard:
Iiiiiiiiiiiiiinnnnn, oooooooonnnnnn,
We streeeetched out the words.
In-on-in-on
Say it fast, that was fun!
Say it fast, now we're done.

Song 3.
Letter Shapes: i, f, n

Verse
i is a stick with a dot that glows;
f has a belt; the top's bent like those.
n is nifty; bend down to your toes;
Grab it, nab it, hang on your nose.

Chorus
i, f, n
i, f, n
i, f, n
Grab it, nab it, hang on your nose!

Episode 2

(Opt.) Fletcher's Birthday Song

Fletcher's a dog who loves to goof around,
Walk on the bed, sleep on the ground.
When you try to hike, he rides along on a bike!
He helps us learn the sounds: a, m, o, i
So he's a dog we like!

Chorus
It's your birthday, happy birthday!
Surprise! It's your birthday, Fletcher's birthday!

Song 4.
Look Up, Top-Down, Left to Right: Start Here

Chorus
Look up, top down, left to right,
Start here,
End there,
Out of sight.
(REPEAT)

Verse
Beginning is the sound at the top of a word;
Ending is the last sound
That you heard.
If you start at the left,
Then you'll end at the right.
I'm reading words
Day and night.
If you start at the left,
Then you'll end at the right.
I'll be reading words
Day and night.
I'll be reading words
Yeah! All right!

Song 5.
Letter Shapes: o, m, a

Verse
o is a shape we make when we yaaaaaawn,
m is a stick with two humps hooked on.
a is a circle in a sort of a way,
With a stick on its side so it can't roll away.

Chorus
o, m, a
o, m, a
o, m, a
is a circle with a stick so it can't roll away!

Lyrics for All Songs

Episode 3

Song 6.
Sneak a Peek, Two Letters at a Time

Sneak a Peek to look ahead;
If you stop in the middle then you won't know what it says.
And if you don't know how it's read, you look ahead
And Sneak a Peek to see what it says.
And Sneak a Peek to see what it says.

Song 7.
Sliding Sound Out

Chorus
Do the Slide—Sliding Sound Out to make two-letter words.
We need ice cream and cookie sounds
to make the word be heard.

Verse
Sound Move the iii, then slide it
Into the nnn sound;
iiinnn! – in!
Is the word you found.

Chorus
Do the Slide—Sliding Sound Out to make two-letter words.
We need ice cream and cookie sounds
to make the word be heard.

Verse
Sound Move the ooo, then slide it
Into the nnn sound;
ooonnn! – on!
Is the word you found.

Verse
Sound Move the iii, then slide it
Into the fff sound;
iiifff! – if!
Is the word you found.

Episode 4

Song 8.
Letter Shapes: u, j, l, s

Verse
u is a cup, fill it up, up, up!
j is a jump with a dot on top;
l looks like a leg when it's turned this way;
s is a snake that slithers away.

Chorus
u, j, l, s
u, j, l, s
u, j, l, s
s is a snake that slithers away!

Song 9.
In Our Own Special Way

Chorus
We all remember things in our own special way.

Verse
Some remember things by the sounds that they say,
Some remember things with a picture in their mind,
Some like to touch a thing to remember what they find.

Chorus
We all remember things in our own special way.

Verse
Some remember morning is when we start the day,
Some remember ducks because they listen for the quacks,
Some remember dogs by the soft fur on their backs.

Chorus
We all remember things in our own special way.
We all remember things in our own special way.

Verse
By looking or picturing or listening for the sounds
Or by moving or thinking through all that we have found.
Or by moving or thinking through all that we have found.

Lyrics for All Songs

Episode 4

Song 10.
That's What Makes the Words Go 'Round

Chorus
That's what makes the words go 'round,
Slide their movements and say their sounds.
That's what makes the words go 'round,
Sound Movements and their sounds.

Verse
Start on the left and ready, set, go!
Slide the movements so they flow.
End on the right, read the words you know
And from left to right we go!

Chorus
That's what makes the words go 'round,
Slide their movements and say their sounds.
That's what makes the words go 'round,
Sound Movements and their sounds.

Verse
Beginning is the first sound that you hear;
The middle sound is very near.
The end is the last sound, I hope that's clear,
From left to right we go!

Chorus
Sound Movements and their sounds.
Sound Movements and their sounds!

Episode 5

Song 11.
Letter Shapes: v, z, r

Verse
v has two sticks, it's the pointy type,
z like a zebra has zig-zag stripes,
r is a stick with a claw sticking out,
Really rip roaring is how the r shouts.

Chorus
Vvv, zzz, give me the rrrrrr!
Vvv, zzz, give me the rrrrrr!
Vvv, zzz, give me the rrrrrr!
Rrrrreally rip roaring is how the rrrrr shouts.

Song 12.
Snap Sound: t

Chorus
Snap sounds in,
Snap sounds out,
They won't let us stretch them out.
Snap sounds short,
Snap sounds fast,
They won't let us stretch them out.

Verse
Snap sounds are the fastest sounds around,
Snap sounds snap right in and snap right out.
Snap!
t snaps in,
t snaps out,
t won't let us stretch it out.
Snap t short,
Snap t fast,
t won't let us stretch it out.
Snap sounds are the fastest sounds around,
Snap sounds snap right in and snap right out.
Snap!

Chorus
Snap sounds in,
Snap sounds out,
They won't let us stretch them out.
Snap sounds short,
Snap sounds fast,
They won't let us stretch them out.

Lyrics for All Songs

Episode 5

Song 13.
Sneak a Peek, Three Letters at a Time

Sneak a Peek along the line,
Take a big breath; say three sounds at a time.
Finger Slide the letters, three by three;
A three-letter word is what it will be!
A three-letter word is what it will be!

Song 14.
Clown Sounds: the Word a

Chorus
Some letters just clown around, clown around,
not saying their sounds,
Some letters just clown around, and disguise
themselves in some way.

Verse
The word a (uh) clowns around, clowns around,
not saying its sound
Like the word a (uh), when it's by itself, it just
likes to play.

Chorus
Some letters just clown around, clown around,
not saying their sounds
Like the word a (uh), when it's by itself, it just
likes to play.
It just likes to play.
It just likes to play. (Fade out.)

Episode 6

Song 15.
Capitals and Periods

Open up the book and turn on the light,
Start on the left and read to your right.
A capital is tall and starts the sentence off,
A period is a dot that makes the sentence stop.
In between the cap and period, there are the
lowercase;
Finger Slide the phrases so they'll be in their
place!

Song 16.
Sneak a Peek, Two Words at a Time

Sneak a Peek, two words at a time,
A two-word phrase sounds just fine.
I'll Finger Slide the words, two by two,
I'm reading phrases I never knew!
I'm reading phrases I never knew!

Lyrics for All Songs

Song 17.
Short Vowels

Verse
Vowels give flavor to every word;
Jump up! Say them so you're heard!

Chorus
a, e, i, o, u   a, e, i, o, u

Verse
Ice-cream vowels, there are five.
Ice-cream vowels, they come alive.

Chorus
a, e, i, o, u   a, e, i, o, u

Verse
There are five short vowels we need to read,
They're like five flavors of ice-cream, yuuummy!
Chorus

Song 18.
Snap Sounds: p, d, g

Chorus
Snap sounds in, snap sounds out,
They won't let us stretch them out.
Snap sounds short, snap sounds fast,
They won't let us stretch them out.

Verse
Snap sounds are the fastest sounds around;
Snap sounds snap right in and snap right out.
Snap!
p snaps in, d snaps out,
g won't let us stretch it out.
Snap p short, Snap d fast,
g won't let us stretch it out.
Snap sounds are the fastest sounds around;
Snap sounds snap right in and snap right out.
Snap!

Chorus
Snap sounds in, snap sounds out,
They won't let us stretch them out.
Snap sounds short, snap sounds fast,
They won't let us stretch them out. Letters, three by three;
A three-letter word is what it will be!
A three-letter word is what it will be!

Song 19.
Monster Words

Verse
A Monster word has letters
That mixes all the sounds.
If you mix up all the letters,
There's a Monster word around.
Like a foll, or a zup, or a creepy crawly po!

Chorus
We can make a Monster word
With all the letters that we know.
We can make a Monster word
With all the letters that we know.

Verse
We can make a Monster word,
We can draw a monster shape,
And the Monster sound it makes
Can be our Monster word's name.
Like a sol, or a pock
Or an icky, wicky wo!

Chorus
We can make a Monster word
With all the letters that we know.
We can make a Monster word
With all the letters that we know.

Clown Sounds: I and TV
(Not shown in video: Use same melody as Song 14 Clown Sounds: the Word a.)

Chorus
Some letters just clown around, clown around, not saying their sounds;
Like the words I and TV – they just like to play.

Verse
The words I and TV clown around by saying their names.
The words I and TV have letters that like to play.

Chorus
Some letters just clown around, clown around, not saying their sounds;
Like the words I and TV – they just like to play.

Verse
The word TV (tee vee) clowns around, clowns around, not saying its sound.
Like the word I (eye), when it's by itself, it just likes to play.

Lyrics for All Songs

Episode 8

Song 20.
Snap Sounds: b, c, k

Chorus
Snap sounds in,
Snap sounds out,
They won't let us stretch them out.
Snap sounds short,
Snap sounds fast,
They won't let us stretch them out.
Snap sounds are the fastest sounds around;
Snap sounds snap right in and snap right out.
Snap!

Verse
b snaps in, c snaps out,
k won't let us stretch it out.
Snap b short, Snap c fast,
k won't let us stretch it out.
Snap sounds are the fastest sounds around;
Snap sounds snap right in and snap right out.
Snap!

Song 21.
Clown Sounds: no, so, go, he, be, me

Chorus
Some letters just clown around, clown around,
not saying their sounds;
Some letters just clown around and disguise
themselves in some way.

Verse (see Note)
No, so, and go, be, and me clown around, not
saying their sounds;
No, so, and go, be, and me have vowels that like
to play.
Some letters just clown around, clown around,
not saying their sounds;
No, so, and go, be, *and me have vowels that like
to play.
They have vowels that like to play.
They have vowels that like to play.
They have vowels that like to play.

Note: The full song lyrics are: "No, so, go, he, be, me have vowels that like to play." Substitute the word "and" for "he" until students learn /h/ in the next program.

Episode 9

Song 22.
Tricky Letters: h, y, w, qu, x

Intro
Tricky letter shapes make tricky letter sounds;
Tricky letter sounds
Try to trick us all the time. (REPEAT)

Verse
h is your breath when your voice isn't there,
w is the wind, blows your feet in the air,
y is the sound you make when you smile,
Tricky sounds trick us all the time.

Verse
qu is the snap shut beak of a duck,
x is the fingers that you cross for good luck,
y is the sound you make when you smile,
Tricky sounds trick us all the time.

Song 23.
Clown Sounds: is, as, his, has

Chorus
Some letters just clown around, clown around,
not saying their sounds.
Some letters just clown around, and disguise
themselves in some way.

Verse
Is and as, his and has clown around, not saying
their sounds.
Is and as, his and has, the s just likes to play.
Some letters just clown around, clown around,
not saying their sounds.
Is and as, his and has, the s just likes to play.
The s just likes to play
The s just likes to play.

Song 24.
"Who" Questions

Verse
Who is the person who teaches every day?
Who is your friend when you go out to play?
Who makes dinner, who takes out the trash?
People do, that's who.

Verse
Who has a doghouse in magic letter land?
Who plays and digs in the dirt and the sand?
Who's called a mutt and who loves to run around?
Fletcher the dog, that's who.

Verse
Who is a person unique in every way?
Who dreams your dreams, who says what you say?
Who's reading words just like you knew you would?
You do! That's who.
You do! That's who.

Episode 10

Song 25.

Chorus
Letter names are crazy,
They make no sense at all.
Letter names are crazy,
They make no sense at all.
Some start with the sound,
Some end with the sound,
Others, they make no sense at all.

Verse 1
Vowels!
/a/ is called ay, /e/ is eee,
/i/ is called eye, /o/ is oh,
/u/ is called ewe, you know it's true,
Letter names they make no sense at all.

Start with the sound!
/k/ is called kay, /j/ is jay,
/b/ is called bee and /d/ is dee,
/p/ is called pea and /t/ is tee,
/v/ is called vee and /z/ is zee.

Chorus
Letter names are crazy,
They make no sense at all.
Letter names are crazy,
They make no sense at all.
Some start with the sound,
Some end with the sound,
Others, they make no sense at all.

Verse 2
End with the sound!
/f/ is called ef, /l/is el,
/m/ is called em, and /n/ is en,
/s/ is called es, /x/ is ex, r is called are.

Crazy letters !
/q/ is called kew, /w/ is double u,
/h/ is called aiche, and /y/ is why,
/g/ is called gee and /c/ is cee.
Letter names, they make no sense at all.

Chorus
Letter names are crazy,
They make no sense at all.
Letter names are crazy,
They make no sense at all.
Some start with the sound,
Some end with the sound,
Others, they make no sense at all.

Song 26.
"Where" Questions

Verse 1
Where are you standing with slippers on your feet?
Where are you sitting with something to eat?
Where is the kitchen and where is the rug?
In a house, that's where.

Verse 2
Where are you standing when you feel a breeze?
Where are the clouds and the mountains and the trees?
Where are the rivers and where is the grass?
Outside, that's where.

Verse 3
Where are the buildings that go way up high?
Where are the stores with things that you buy?
Where are the schools where you learn to read?
In the city, that's where.
In the city, that's where.

Song 27.
Clown Sounds: the, to, do, my, by

Chorus
Some letters just clown around, clown around, not saying their sounds;
Some letters just clown around and disguise themselves in some way.

Verse
The, to, do, my and by clown around, not saying their sounds.
The, to, do, my and by have vowels that like to play.
Some letters just clown around, clown around, not saying their sounds;
The, to, do, my and by have vowels that like to play.
They have vowels that like to play
They have vowels that like to play
They have vowels that like to play.

Sound Movements for Quick Reference for All Letters

Learn the Open Reading sound movements for the alphabet plus the first "partner" sound.

Watch the Fletcher's Place episodes with your child to learn the sound movements, or have your child teach them to you!

Sound Movements for Quick Reference

Sound movement images and descriptions are included for each letter as memory hooks. These movements help children remember the main sound for each letter and help blend sounds together to smoothly read and spell words.

Learn the Open Reading open source sound movements and main sound for each of the 26 letters and one "partner letter" sound, while watching the videos with children.

a

Open your right hand wide. Move it from left to right and open your mouth wide while saying the sound "aaaaa."

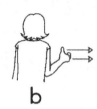

b

Make a fist with your right hand. Raise your thumb in the shape of the b. Move your hand from left to right as if "bumping a belly," while quickly saying the sound "b!"

c

Imagine "crushing a can" in your fist while quickly saying the sound "c!"

d

Make a fist with your right hand and lift your thumb up in the shape of the d. Hold it still and say, "Don't let the donut roll!" and quickly say the sound "d!"

e

Start with an open flat hand, palm down. Flip it over to show the hand is "eeempty" while saying the sound "eeeee."

f

Make a fanning motion by sweeping your open flat hand in front of your face. Place top teeth on lower lip while saying the airy sound "fffff."

g

Bend your elbows placing your fingers at your waist. Pretend to be a gorilla and quickly say the sound "g!"

h

Hold your hand in front of your mouth. Breathe out hot air while saying the airy sound "hhhhh."

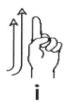

i

Bring your pointer finger up as if you had stuck it in something icky, while saying the sound "iiiii."

Sound Movements for Quick Reference

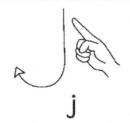

j

Imagine your pointer finger is skateboarding down and then up the letter shape while saying the sound "jjjj."

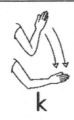

k

Hold out a stiff hand and make a karate chop in the air while quickly saying the sound "k!"

ck

Imagine crushing a can with your fist, then open your hand to do a karate chop saying the sound "ck."

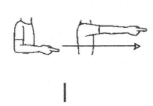

l

Move your pointer finger away from your body while saying, "Look, a lion!" and then say the sound "lllll!"

m

With an open hand, rub your tummy in a circle. Think of something yummy and with lips closed say the sound "mmmmm."

n

Curve fingers and thumb over your nose in the shape of the letter *n*. Point your tongue up toward your nose and with lips open say the sound "nnnnn."

o

Curve your hand into a circle and hold it "oooon" your mouth while saying the sound "ooooo."

p

Imagine pulling down on the tail of the letter *p* with your thumb and pointer finger while making the popping airy sound "p!"

qu

Press four fingers together. As you bring them to your thumb quickly say the sound "q!" (Say the sounds "k w" quickly. Don't add the "uh" sound.)

r

Bend your fingers into a claw. Clamp your back teeth together with lips open while saying the sound "rrrrr."

s

Hold your palm face down. Slither it up and down like a snake while saying the airy sound "sssss."

t

Touch your pointer finger to your thumb. Flick it like flicking a bug away while saying the airy sound "t."

Sound Movements for Quick Reference

u

Cup your hand in the shape of the letter *u*. Move your hand up while saying the sound "uuuuu."

v

Make a victory or peace sign in the shape of the letter *v* while saying the sound "vvvvv."

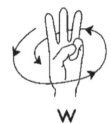

w

Hold up three fingers in the shape of the letter *w*. Whirl them in a circle while saying the sound "wwwww." (Don't add the "uh" sound by dropping your jaw.)

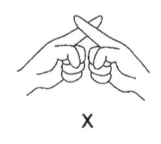

x

Cross both pointer fingers in the shape of the letter *x* while saying the sound "x!" (Say the two letter sounds "k s" quickly.)

y

Use your right thumb and pointer finger to push up the corners of your mouth. Imagine your arm is the tail of the letter *y* while saying the sound "yyyyy." (The letter name "E" is the sound for the letter *y*.)

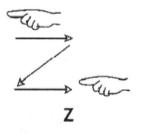

z

Imagine your pointer finger is the "sword of Zorro." Trace the *z* shape in the air while saying the sound "zzzzz."

th

Place your thumb over the top of your fist. Place your tongue slightly out over your bottom teeth while saying the airy sound "th."

Fletcher's Place Left-to-Right Reading Arrows

-In Episodes 4-10 children train their eyes to read from left to right.

-Before beginning Episode 4, cut out a reading arrow. (For a sturdier arrow, glue it to cardboard.)
 Children use it to read letters, words, phrases and sentences.

-To use, place the arrow with the dog's head on the left under individual letters, words,
 phrases, and sentences. Children slide their pointer finger along the arrow from
 the dog to the bone as they read to guide their eyes from left to right along the text.

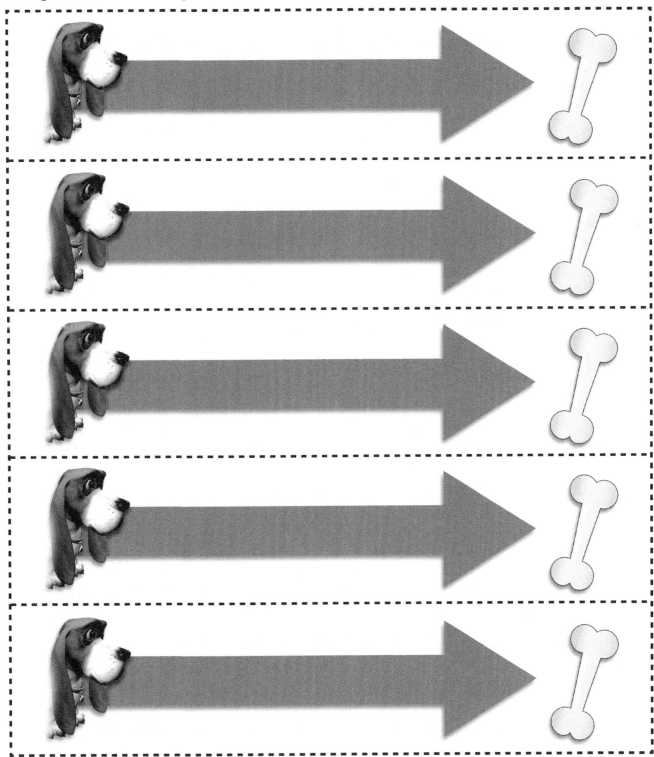